AAT

Financial Accounting: Preparing Financial Statements

Pocket Notes

These Pocket Notes support study for the following AAT qualifications:

AAT Level 3 Diploma in Accounting

AAT Level 3 Certificate in Bookkeeping

AAT Diploma in Accounting at SCQF Level 7

British library cataloguing-in-publication data

A catalogue record for this book is available from the British Library.

Published by:
Kaplan Publishing UK
Unit 2 The Business Centre
Molly Millars Lane
Wokingham
Berkshire
RG41 2QZ

ISBN 978-1-83996-602-6

Printed and bound in Great Britain.

Contents

		Study text chapter	Page Number
A guide to the assessment			1
Chapter 1	Double-entry bookkeeping	1	5
Chapter 2	Accounting for VAT and payroll	2	17
Chapter 3	Capital and revenue expenditure	3	25
Chapter 4	Depreciation	4	31
Chapter 5	Disposal of capital assets	5	41
Chapter 6	Extended trial balance – an introduction	6	51
Chapter 7	Underlying accounting principles	7	55
Chapter 8	Accounting for inventory	8	61
Chapter 9	Irrecoverable and doubtful debts	9	69
Chapter 10	Control account reconciliations	10	81
Chapter 11	Bank reconciliations	11	95
Chapter 12	Accruals and prepayments	12	97
Chapter 13	Suspense accounts and errors	13	107
Chapter 14	Extended trial balance – in action	14	117
Chapter 15	Sole trader accounts	15	131

Chapter 16	Partnership accounts	16	149
Chapter 17	Incomplete records	17	159
Chapter 18	Interpretation of profitability ratios	18	183
Index			I.1

Preface

These Pocket Notes contain the key points you need to know for the exam, presented in a unique visual way that makes revision easy and effective.

Written by experienced lecturers and authors, these Pocket Notes break down content into manageable chunks to maximise your concentration.

Quality and accuracy are of the utmost importance to us so if you spot an error in any of our products, please send an email to mykaplanreporting@kaplan.com with full details, or follow the link to the feedback form in MyKaplan.

Our Quality Co-ordinator will work with our technical team to verify the error and take action to ensure it is corrected in future editions.

A guide to the assessment

The assessment

Financial Accounting: Preparing Financial Statements (FAPS) is the financial accounting unit studied on the Diploma in Professional Accounting.

Examination

FAPS is assessed by means of a computer based assessment. The CBA will last for two and a half hours and consists of 6 tasks.

In any one assessment, students may not be assessed on all content, or on the full depth or breadth of a piece of content. The content assessed may change over time to ensure validity of assessment, but all assessment criteria will be tested over time.

Learning outcomes & weighting

Learning outcome	Weighting
1. Understand the accounting principles underlying final accounts preparation	5%
2. Understand the principles of advanced double-entry bookkeeping	10%
3. Implement procedures for the acquisition and disposal of non-current assets	10%
4. Prepare and record depreciation calculations	10%
5. Record period end adjustments	10%
6. Produce and extend the trial balance	15%
7. Produce the financial statements for sole traders and partnerships	20%
8. Interpret financial statements using profitability ratios	10%
9. Prepare accounting records from incomplete information	10%
Total	100%

Pass mark

To pass a unit assessment, students need to achieve a mark of 70% or more.

This unit contributes 40% of the total amount required for the Diploma in Professional Accounting.

chapter

1

Double-entry bookkeeping

- Principles of double-entry bookkeeping.
- Accounting equation.
- Ledger accounts.
- General rules of double-entry bookkeeping.
- Accounting for cash transactions.
- Accounting for credit transactions.
- Balancing ledger accounts.
- Preparing a trial balance.

Principles of double-entry bookkeeping

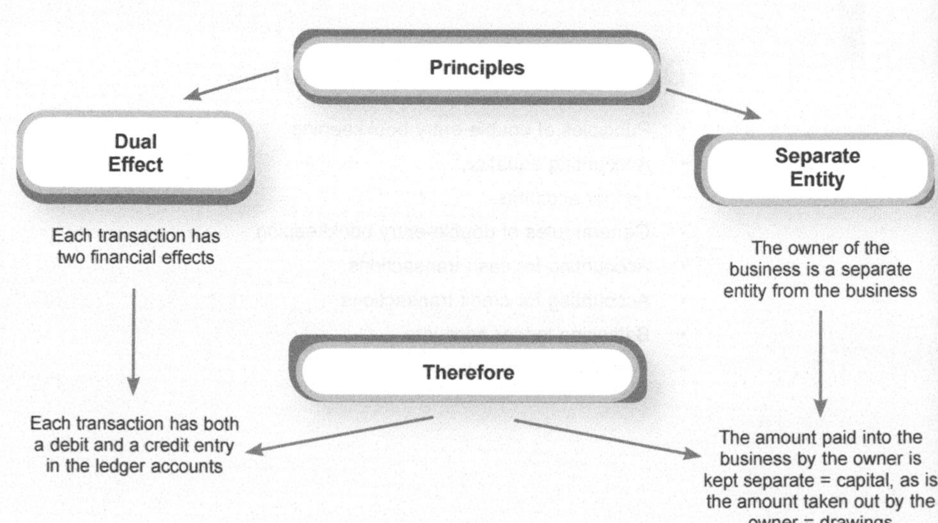

Accounting equation

Assets – Liabilities = Capital

Terminology

Asset
Something owned by the business

Liability
Something owed by the business

Capital
Amount the owner has invested in the business

Receivable
Someone who owes the business money

Payable
Someone the business owes money to

Ledger accounts

Typical ledger account:

Title of account

Date	Narrative	£	Date	Narrative	£
	Debit side	x		**Credit** side	x

The dual effect means that every transaction is recorded as a debit in one account and a credit in another account.

Key question – which account is the debit entry to and which account is the credit entry to?

General rules of double-entry bookkeeping

Ledger account

Debit	**Credit**
Money in	Money out
Increase in asset	Increase in liability
Decrease in liability	Decrease in asset
Increase in expense	Increase in income

Accounting for cash transactions

Examples of ledger accounting:

(i) Payment of £10,000 into business bank account by owner:

Debit Cash (money in)

Credit Capital (increase in liability – amount owed to owner)

Cash account

	£		£
Capital	10,000		

Capital account

	£		£
		Cash	10,000

(ii) Purchase of goods for cash of £3,000:

Debit Purchases (expense)

Credit Cash (money out)

Purchases account

	£		£
Cash	3,000		

Cash account

	£		£
		Purchases	3,000

Accounting for credit transactions

(i) Purchases goods for £6,000 on credit

Debit Purchases (expense)

Credit Trade Payables (liability)

Purchases account

	£		£
Trade payables	6,000		

Trade payables account

	£		£
		Purchases	6,000

(ii) Sale of goods on credit for £8,000

Debit Trade Receivables (asset)

Credit Sales Revenue (income)

Trade receivables account

	£		£
Sales	8,000		

Sales account

	£		£
		Trade receivables	8,000

(iii) Payment of part of money owed to credit supplier of £1,500

Debit Trade payables (reduction in liability)

Credit Cash (money out)

Trade payables account

	£		£
Cash	1,500		

Cash account

	£		£
		Trade payables	1,500

(iv) Receipt of part of money owed by credit customer of £5,000

Debit Cash (money in)

Credit Trade receivables (reduction in asset)

Cash account

	£		£
Trade receivables	5,000		

Trade receivables account

	£		£
		Cash	5,000

Balancing ledger accounts

At various points in time the owner/owners of a business will need information about the total transactions in the period. Eg, total sales, amount of payables outstanding, amount of cash remaining. This can be found by balancing the ledger accounts.

Here is a typical cash (or bank) account:

Cash account

	£		£
Capital	10,000	Purchases	3,000
Sales	4,000	Rent	500
Receivables	5,000	Payables	1,500

Step 1 Total both debit and credit side and make a note of the totals.

Step 2 Insert higher of totals as total for both sides (leaving a line before inserting totals).

Cash account

	£		£
Capital	10,000	Purchases	3,000
Sales	4,000	Rent	500
Receivables	5,000	Payables	1,500
	19,000		19,000

Step 3 On side with smaller total insert figure which makes it add up to total and call this the balance carried down (balance c/d).

Cash account

	£		£
Capital	10,000	Purchases	3,000
Sales	4,000	Rent	500
Receivables	5,000	Payables	1,500
		Balance c/d	14,000
	19,000		19,000

Step 4 On the opposite side of the account enter this same figure below the total line and call it the balance brought down (balance b/d).

Cash account

	£		£
Capital	10,000	Purchases	3,000
Sales	4,000	Rent	500
Receivables	5,000	Payables	1,500
		Balance c/d	14,000
	19,000		19,000
Balance b/d	14,000		

This shows that after all of these transactions there is £14,000 of cash left as an asset in the business (a debit balance = an asset).

CBA focus

In the assessment you will be required to balance a number of ledger accounts.

Preparing a trial balance

What is a trial balance?

- list of all of the ledger balances in the general ledger
- debit balances and credit balances are listed separately
- debit balance total should equal credit balance total.

Example

Simple trial balance

	Debit £	Credit £
Sales		5,000
Wages	100	
Purchases	3,000	
Rent	200	
Vehicle	3,000	
Receivables	100	
Payables		1,400
	6,400	6,400

Debit or credit balance?

If you are just given a list of balances you must know whether they are debit or credit balances.

Remember the rules!

Debit Balances	Credit Balances
Assets	Liabilities
Expenses	Income

Sales and purchases returns

Sales returns = debit balance (opposite to sales)

Purchases returns = credit balance (opposite to purchases)

Discounts allowed and discounts received

Discounts allowed = debit balance (expense)

Discounts received = credit balance (opposite of an expense)

CBA focus

Returns and discounts are not as obvious as other accounts as to whether they are debit or credit balances so make sure that you understand the logic behind these balances.

chapter

2

Accounting for VAT and payroll

- What is VAT?
- Rates of VAT.
- Calculation of VAT.
- Accounting for VAT.
- Payroll.

What is VAT?

- tax on consumer expenditure
- collected by HM Revenue and Customs (HMRC) as goods are bought and sold during the supply chain
- VAT-registered business charges VAT on sales (output tax) and incurs VAT on purchases (input tax)
- difference between the output tax and the input tax is the amount due to or from HMRC.

Rates of VAT

- different rates of VAT apply to different types of supplies.

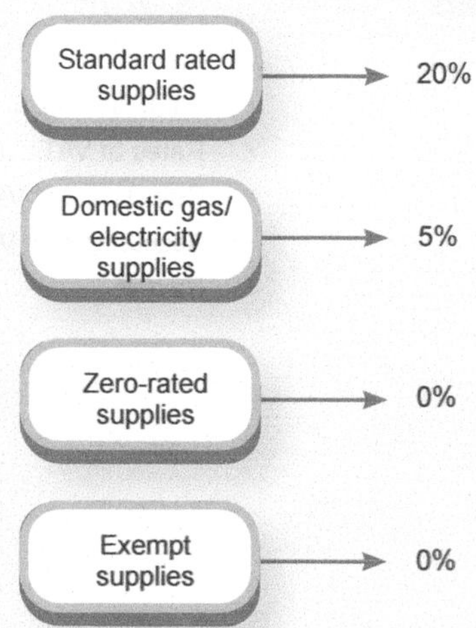

Zero-rated v Exempt

Zero rated	0%	If zero-rated goods are sold, VAT on purchases can still be recovered
Exempt	0%	If exempt supplies are sold, no VAT can be recovered on purchases – VAT becomes additional cost of business

Calculation of VAT

Example

Goods are sold for £1,000 exclusive (net) of VAT:

VAT = £1,000 x 20% = £200

Total value = £1,000 + £200 = £1,200

Goods are purchased for £600 inclusive of VAT (gross):

VAT = £600 x 20/120 = £100

Net value = £600 – £100 = £500

Example

Goods are sold for £2,000 exclusive (net) of VAT:

VAT = £2,000 x 20% = £400

Total value = £2,000 + £400 = £2,400

Goods are purchased for £900 inclusive of VAT (gross):

VAT = £900 x 20/120 = £150

Net value = £900 – £150 = £750

CBA focus

In the assessment you often have to calculate VAT on both sales/purchases/income/expenses which are exclusive (net) of VAT and sales/purchases which are inclusive of VAT (gross).

Accounting for VAT

- VAT on sales and purchases are normally recorded in the sales day book and purchases day book
- postings made from these books of prime entry to the ledger accounts

Example

Sales day book	Total	VAT	Net
	£	£	£
Total	36,000	6,000	30,000
	Debit	Credit	Credit
	RLCA as amount owed by receivables	VAT a/c as amount owed to HMRC	Sales a/c as net amount of sale
Purchases day book	Total	VAT	Net
	£	£	£
Total	19,200	3,200	16,000
	Credit	Debit	Debit
	PLCA as amount owed to payables	VAT a/c as amount due back from HMRC	Purchases a/c as net amount of purchases

Sales account

	£		£
		RLCA	30,000

Receivables ledger control account

	£		£
Sales	36,000		

VAT control account

	£		£
PLCA	3,200	RLCA	6,000

Purchases account

	£		£
PLCA	16,000		

Payables ledger control account

	£		£
		Purchases	19,200

When all of the transactions for a quarter have been recorded, the VAT control account can be balanced to determine the amount due to or from HMRC.

VAT control account

	£		£
PLCA	3,200	RLCA	6,000
Balance c/d	2,800		
	6,000		6,000
		Balance b/d	2,800

This means that £2,800 is due to be paid to HMRC as it is a credit balance (liability).

This amount will have to be paid to HMRC – double entry:

Debit	VAT control account	£2,800
Credit	Bank account	£2,800

Debit balance on VAT account

If the balance b/d was a debit balance (asset), this would mean that the amount was due back from HMRC. When this VAT refund is received from HMRC, the double entry is:

Debit Bank account

Credit VAT control account

CBA focus

In the assessment you might be required to post the day books including the VAT.

You might also have to deal with errors that involve VAT so you need to understand the double entry.

Accounting for VAT

- sales shown net of VAT in SPL
- if VAT is recoverable, purchases/ expenses shown net of VAT in SPL
- if VAT is irrecoverable, VAT is included in purchases/expenses in SPL
- VAT due to/from HMRC shown in statement of financial position as liability/ asset.

Payroll

Overview of the payroll function

The responsibilities of payroll staff within an organisation include:

- calculating correctly the amount of pay due to each employee,
- ensuring each employee is paid on time with the correct amount,
- ensuring amounts due to external parties such as HM Revenue and Customs are correctly determined and paid on time.

Gross pay

Gross pay is the wage or salary due to the employee for the amount of work done in the period.

Net pay

Net pay is the amount that the employee will actually receive after appropriate deductions have been made.

PAYE

The PAYE scheme is a national scheme whereby employers withhold tax and other deductions from their employees' wages and salaries when they are paid. The deductions are then paid over monthly to HM Revenue and Customs by the employer.

National insurance

National Insurance is a state scheme run by HM Revenue and Customs which pays certain benefits including; retirement pensions, widow's allowances and pensions, jobseeker's allowance, incapacity benefit and maternity allowance. The scheme is funded by people who are currently in employment and have earnings above a certain level.

Accounting entries for wages and salaries

Payroll transactions are recorded by journal entries which traces the accounting entry from the payroll record to the journal book to being entered into the general ledger.

The accounting entries for wages and salaries are as follows:

1. Dr Wages expense account Cr Wages and salaries control account with the total expenses relating to the business (gross pay plus employer's NIC)

2. Dr Wages and salaries control account Cr Bank account with the net wages paid to the employees

3. Dr Wages and salaries control account Cr HMRC liability with those deductions made from the employees which are payable to the HM Revenue and Customs

If applicable it may also be necessary to record a payable to the pension fund and any other voluntary deductions that are made.

4. Dr Wages and salaries control account Cr Pension / Other voluntary deduction liability with those deductions made from the employees which are payable to the pension fund or other voluntary deduction.

chapter

3

Capital and revenue expenditure

- IAS 16 Property, plant and equipment.
- Capital and revenue expenditure.
- Financing purchases of property, plant and equipment.
- Recording the purchase of non-current assets.
- Tangible and intangible non-current assets.

IAS 16 Property, plant and equipment

- covers accounting treatment of tangible non-current assets and depreciation.

Non-current assets = Long-term assets of the business

Tangible non-current assets = Long-term assets with physical form

Capital and revenue expenditure

Capital expenditure

- expenditure to acquire/enhance economic benefits of non-current assets
- recorded in statement of financial position

Revenue expenditure

- all other expenditure
- charged to statement of profit or loss

Accounting for capital expenditure

Initial purchase:

Debit	Non-current asset account
Credit	Bank account/payables account with cost of non-current asset

Financing purchases of property, plant and equipment.

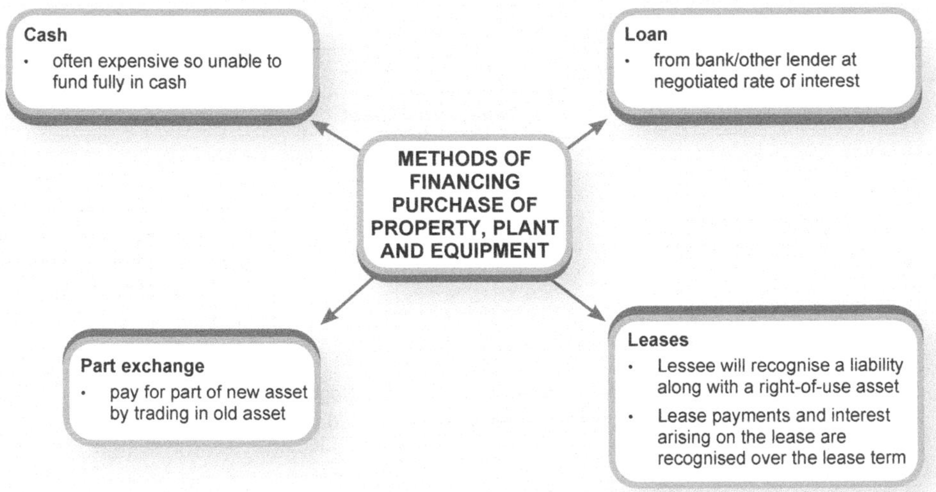

Recording the purchase of non-current assets

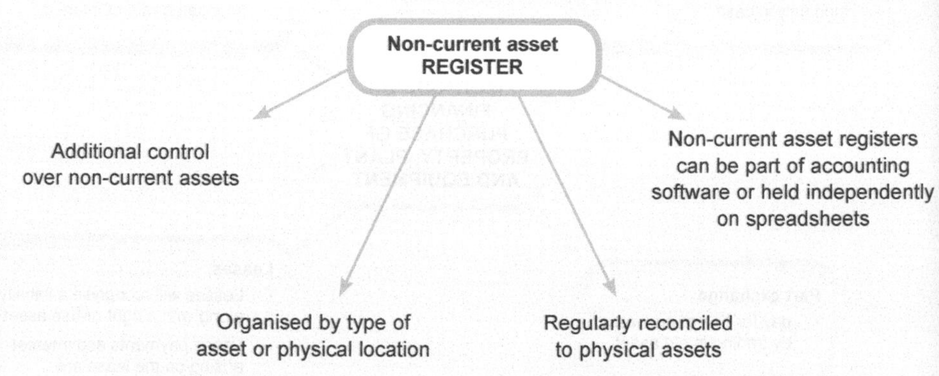

Typical layout

Non-current asset register – motor vehicles

Description/ serial number	Date acquired	Cost	Depreciation	Carrying amount	Funding method	Disposal proceeds	Disposal date
		£	£	£		£	
Ford Mondeo							
GN02 HGG	01/03/X2	16,000			Part-ex		
Y/e 31/12/X2			3,200	12,800			
Y/e 31/12/X3			2,560	10,240			
Honda Accord							
GN03 JFD	01/01/X3	18,000			Cash		
Y/e 31/12/X3			3,600	14,400			

- when an asset is purchased, as well as being recorded in the ledger account, it will also be recorded in the non-current asset register.

Tangible and intangible non-current assets

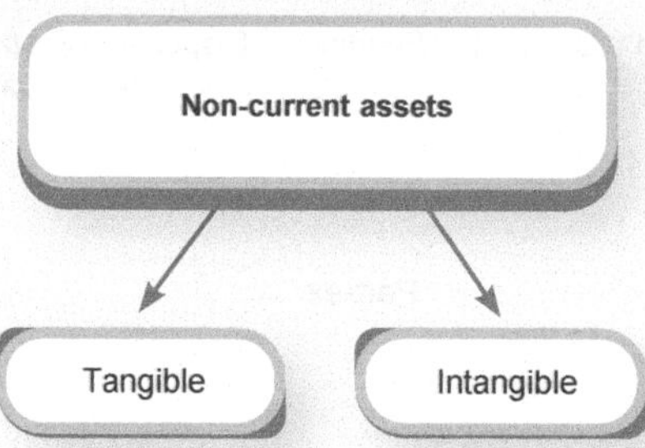

Tangible

- physical form e.g. plant and machinery
- included in statement of financial position

Intangible

- no physical form e.g. goodwill
- often not included in statement of financial position

chapter

4

Depreciation

- What is depreciation?
- Calculating the depreciation charge.
- Accounting for depreciation charge.
- Calculating and recording depreciation charge.

What is depreciation?

Definition of depreciation

- measure of the cost of the economic benefits of non-current assets that have been consumed during the period
- consumption includes wearing out, using up or other reduction in the useful economic life of the non-current asset whether arising from use, effluxion of time or obsolescence.

Aim of depreciation

- for the expenditure on a non-current asset to be matched against the income generated by the asset throughout its useful economic life to the business.

Accounting concept relating to depreciation

- accruals concept.

CBA focus

It is important that you realise that the purpose of depreciation is in accordance with the accruals concept and to spread the cost of the asset over the period in which it is being used within the business.

Calculating the depreciation charge

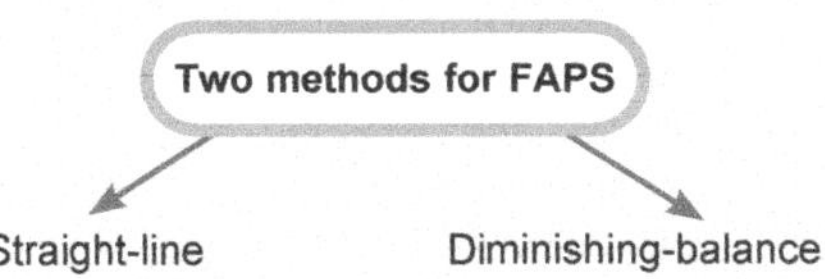

Depreciation can be calculated automatically by accounting software or independently through spreadsheets.

Straight-line method

$$\text{Annual depreciation charge} = \frac{\text{(Cost – residual value)}}{\text{Useful life}}$$

OR

(Cost – residual value) x %

This is a fixed percentage applied.

Definition

Residual value

- current estimate of sale/scrap value at the end of the useful life.

Useful life

- period over which the business will derive economic benefit from the asset.

Example

Machine purchased for £20,000 on 1 January 20X4. Expected to be used for 5 years with an anticipated scrap value at the end of that period of £6,500.

Solution

$$\text{Annual charge} = \frac{(£20{,}000 - 6{,}500)}{5 \text{ years}}$$

$$= £2{,}700$$

- same charge in each year of the asset's life.

Diminishing-balance method

- fixed percentage applied to carrying amount
- carrying amount = cost less accumulated depreciation.

Example

Machine purchased for £20,000 on 1 January 20X4. Depreciation is at 20% per annum on the diminishing-balance basis.

Solution

Charge for 20X4 = £20,000 x 20%
= £4,000

Charge for 20X5 = (£20,000 – £4,000) x 20%
= £3,200

Charge for 20X6 = (£20,000 - £4,000 - £3,200) x 20%
= £2,560

- depreciation charge is higher in early years of asset's life and lower in later years
- particularly suits assets such as motor vehicles for which higher benefits are consumed in the earlier years with reducing benefits as the years of use pass by.

Accounting for depreciation charge

Depreciation charge – two effects:

Expense in the statement of profit or loss	Reduction in value of asset in statement of financial position

Double entry:

Debit	Depreciation charge account
Credit	Accumulated depreciation account

Machine purchased for £20,000 on 1 January 20X4.Expected to be used for 5 years with an anticipated scrap value at the end of that period of £6,500.

Straight-line depreciation is to be used.

Solution

Step 1

Calculate annual depreciation charge:

$$\text{Annual charge} = \frac{(£20,000 - 6,500)}{5 \text{ years}}$$

$$= £2,700$$

Step 2

Open up depreciation charge account and accumulated depreciation account.

Depreciation charge account

£	£

Accumulated depreciation account

£	£

Step 3

Put through the double entry for 20X4:

Debit	Depreciation charge account	£2,700
Credit	Accumulated depreciation account	£2,700

Depreciation charge account

	£		£
Accumulated depreciation	2,700		

Accumulated depreciation account

	£		£
		Depreciation charge	2,700

Step 4

Balance the accounts:

- depreciation charge is transferred to the statement of profit or loss as an expense
- accumulated depreciation balance is shown on statement of financial position.

Depreciation charge account

	£		£
Accumulated depreciation	2,700	SPL	2,700
	2,700		2,700

Accumulated depreciation account

	£		£
Balance c/d	2,700	Depreciation charge	2,700
	2,700		2,700
		Balance b/d	2,700

Step 5

Produce statement of financial position entries:

Statement of financial position 31 December 20X4

	Cost	Accum Dep'n	
	£	£	£
Plant and machinery	20,000	(2,700)	17,300

Step 6

Repeat for following year, 20X5:

Depreciation charge account

	£		£
Accumulated depreciation	2,700	SPL	2,700
	2,700		2,700

Accumulated depreciation account

	£		£
		Balance b/d*	2,700
Balance c/d	5,400	Depreciation charge	2,700
	5,400		5,400
		Balance b/d	5,400

* Note that the balance from 20X4 is brought down.

Statement of financial position 31 December 20X5

	Cost	Dep'n	
	£	£	£
Plant and machinery	20,000	(5,400)	14,600

CBA focus

Accounting for non-current assets and depreciation is a large part of the examination and you will have to calculate depreciation charges and update account balances for depreciation using either the straight-line or diminishing-balance method.

Calculating and recording depreciation charge

- each year the depreciation charge is calculated for each asset and recorded in the non-current asset register
- then also recorded in the ledger accounts.

Example

Year ended 31/12/X4

Non-current asset register – motor vehicles

Description/ serial number	Date acquired	Cost £	Depreciation £	Carrying amount £	Funding method	Disposal proceeds £	Disposal date
Ford Mondeo							
GN02 HGG	01/03/X2	16,000			Part-ex		
Y/e 31/12/X2			3,200	12,800			
Y/e 31/12/X3			2,560	10,240			
Y/e 31/12/X4			**2,048**	**8,192**			
Honda Accord							
GN03 JFD	01/01/X3	18,000			Cash		
Y/e 31/12/X3			3,600	14,400			
Y/e 31/12/X4			**2,880**	**11,520**			

CBA focus

In the assessment you will be expected to complete a non-current asset register.

chapter

5

Disposal of capital assets

- Accounting for disposals.
- Part-exchange.
- Recording the disposal of non-current assets.
- Reconciling the non-current asset register to the physical assets.

Accounting for disposals

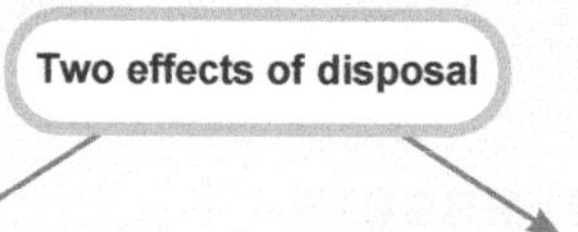

Asset must be removed from statement of financial position

- remove asset at cost
- remove accumulated depreciation

Account for gain or loss on disposal recognised in the statement of profit or loss

- difference between proceeds and carrying amount

Entries made in disposal account

Example

A machine which cost £20,000 is sold for £10,000. Depreciation charge to date on the asset (balance on accumulated depreciation account) is £8,100.

Solution

Step 1

Transfer cost of asset from non-current asset account to disposal account.

Non-current asset account

	£		£
Balance b/d	20,000	Disposal account	20,000

Disposal account

	£		£
Non-current asset – cost	20,000		

Example

Step 2

Transfer accumulated depreciation to disposal account.

Accumulated depreciation account

	£		£
Disposal account	8,100	Balance b/d	8,100

Disposal account

	£		£
Non-current asset – cost	20,000	Accumulated dep'n	8,100

Step 3

Enter disposal proceeds in disposal account

Disposal account

	£		£
Non-current asset – cost	20,000	Accumulated dep'n	8,100
		Bank	10,000

Step 4

Balance disposal account to find gain or loss on disposal and transfer this to the statement of profit or loss.

Disposal account

	£		£
Non-current asset – cost	20,000	Accumulated dep'n	8,100
		Bank	10,000
		Loss on disposal SPL	1,900
	20,000		20,000

Loss on disposal can be checked:

	£
Cost of asset	20,000
Accumulated depreciation	(8,100)
Carrying amount	11,900
Disposal proceeds	(10,000)
Loss on disposal	1,900

Part-exchange

Business

Wants to acquire new asset.

Offers old asset in part-exchange.

Pays for remaining cost of new asset.

Dealer

Agrees to take old asset in part-exchange.

Values old asset and gives part-exchange allowance.

Part-exchange allowance/value

- effectively proceeds of old asset disposal.
- also part of cost of new asset.

Example

A business has a car which cost £15,000 and has accumulated depreciation to date of £10,000. A new car is to be acquired at a total cost of £18,000 but the car dealer will take the old car in part-exchange and give a part-exchange allowance of £3,500.

Solution

Step 1

Transfer cost and accumulated depreciation to the disposal account.

Non-current asset at cost – old car

	£		£
Balance b/d	15,000	Disposal account	15,000

Accumulated depreciation – old car

	£		£
Disposal account	10,000	Balance b/d	10,000

Disposal account

	£		£
Non-current asset cost	15,000	Accumulated Depreciation	10,000

Step 2

Account for purchase of new car – payment is made for the difference between the total cost of £18,000 and the part-exchange allowance of £3,500 – i.e. £14,500.

Non-current asset at cost – new car

	£		£
Bank	14,500		

Example

Step 3

Account for part-exchange allowance:

- in disposal account treat as proceeds
- in non-current asset account treat as part of cost.

Debit	Non-current asset at cost	£3,500
Credit	Disposal account	£3,500

Disposal account

	£		£
Cost	15,000	Depreciation	10,000
		Non-current asset at cost	3,500

Non-current asset at cost – new car

	£		£
Bank	14,500		
Disposal – part-exchange	3,500		

The non-current asset at cost account now shows the full cost of the new car of £18,000.

Step 4

Balance disposal account to find gain/loss on disposal.

Disposal account

	£		£
Cost	15,000	Depreciation	10,000
		Non-current asset at cost	3,500
		Loss on disposal	1,500
	15,000		15,000

CBA focus

In the assessment there may be a disposal of a non-current asset which must be accounted for. In most cases it will have a part-exchange involved as well so you must understand the accounting for this.

Recording the disposal of non-current assets

Example

Year ended 31/12/X5

On 30 June 20X5 the Ford Mondeo is sold for £7,000. The policy is to charge no depreciation in the year of disposal of an asset.

The details must be recorded in the non-current asset register.

Non-current asset register – motor vehicles

Description/ serial number	Date acquired	Cost	Depreciation	Carrying amount	Funding method	Disposal proceeds	Disposal date
		£	£	£		£	
Ford Mondeo							
GN02 HGG	01/03/X2	16,000			Part-ex		
Y/e 31/12/X2			3,200	12,800			
Y/e 31/12/X3			2,560	10,240			
y/e 31/12/X4			2,048	8,192			
y/e 31/12/X5						**7,000**	**(30/6/X5)**

Description/ serial number	Date acquired	Cost £	Depreciation £	Carrying amount £	Funding method	Disposal proceeds £	Disposal date
Honda Accord							
GN03 JFD	01/01/X3	18,000			Cash		
Y/e 31/12/X3			3,600	14,400			
Y/e 31/12/X4			2,880	11,520			
Y/e 31/12/X5			**2,304**	**9,216**			

Reconciling the non-current asset register to the physical assets

- purpose of non-current asset register is control of assets
- on a regular basis the assets recorded in the register must be checked to the physical assets held by the business
- discrepancies must be investigated.

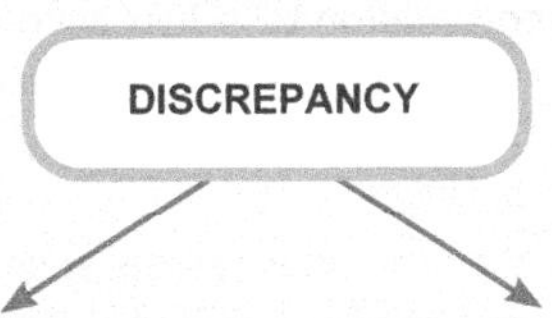

Asset in register but not physically present

- may have been sold but not recorded
- may be in another location
- may have been stolen

Asset on premises but not in register

- register may not be up-to-date
- asset may have been moved from another location

Reconciliation to ledger accounts

- the non-current asset register should also be agreed to the ledger account balances
- the non-current assets at cost ledger account balance should agree to the cost less disposals in the non-current asset register
- the accumulated depreciation ledger account balance should agree to the total of depreciation charges to date in the non-current asset register
- the total gain/loss in disposal column should agree to the amount credited/ charged to statement of profit or loss.

chapter

6

Extended trial balance – an introduction

- Purpose of an extended trial balance.
- Layout of an extended trial balance.

Purpose of an extended trial balance

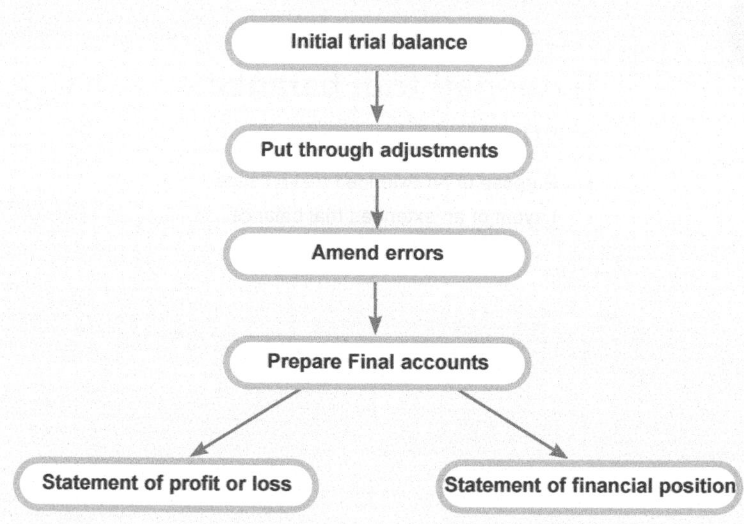

Layout of an extended trial balance

Typical ETB:

Account name	Trial balance		Adjustments		Statement of profit or loss		Statement of financial position	
	DR	CR	DR	CR	DR	CR	DR	CR
	£	£	£	£	£	£	£	£

chapter

7

Underlying accounting principles

- Users of final accounts.
- The framework of accounting underlying the preparation of final accounts.
- Qualities of useful financial information.
- Ethical principles.

Users of final accounts

Investors (Shareholders) use final accounts to make decisions about buying, selling or holding equity in the company.

Lenders use final accounts to decide whether to provide loans or other forms of credit.

Other payables use final accounts to decide whether to supply goods on credit and the terms of the credit.

Management use final accounts to compare the performance of the organisation with that of other organisations in the same business sector.

The framework of accounting underlying the preparation of final accounts

Going concern the entity will continue in operation for the foreseeable future and has neither the need nor the intention to liquidate or significantly reduce the scale of its operations.

Accruals basis transactions should be reflected in the financial statements for the period in which they occur. This means that income should be recognised as it is earned and expenses when they are incurred, rather than when cash is received or paid.

Business entity from an accounting perspective the business is treated as being separate from its owners.

Materiality relates to the significance of transactions, balances and errors that may be within the financial statements.

Consistency transactions and valuation methods are treated the same way from period to period.

Prudence good and careful judgement.

Money measurement an accounting transaction should only be recorded if it can be expressed in terms of money.

Qualities of useful financial information

The framework identifies two fundamental qualitative characteristics of useful financial information. Preparers of the financial information should attempt to maximise these characteristics to benefit the users of the accounts.

Relevance ensures that the information is capable of influencing the decision-making of the users of the financial information.

Faithful representation ensures that the information is complete, neutral and free from error.

There are also four supporting qualitative characteristics:

Comparability – it should be possible to compare an entity over time and with similar information about other entities.

Verifiability – if information can be verified (e.g. through an audit) this provides assurance to the users that it is both credible and reliable.

Timeliness – information should be provided to users within a timescale suitable for their decision making purposes.

Understandability – information should be understandable to those that might want to review and use it. This can be facilitated through appropriate classification, characterisation and presentation of information.

Ethical principles

Ethics can be defined as the "moral principles that govern a person's behaviour or the conducting of an activity".

The Code of Ethics for Professional Accountants, published by The International Federation of Accountants (IFAC), forms the basis for the ethical codes of many accountancy bodies.

Five key principles

Integrity

Integrity means that a member must be straightforward and honest in all professional and business relationships. Integrity also implies fair dealing and truthfulness.

Objectivity

Objectivity means that a member must not allow bias, conflict of interest or undue influence of others to override professional or business judgements.

Professional competence and due care

Professional competence means that a member has a continuing duty to maintain professional knowledge and skill at the level required to ensure that a client or employer receives competent professional service based on current developments in practice, legislation and techniques.

Due care means a member must act diligently and in accordance with applicable technical and professional standards when providing professional services.

Confidentiality

A member must, in accordance with the law, respect the confidentiality of information acquired as a result of professional and business relationships and not disclose any such information to third parties without proper and specific authority unless there is a legal or professional right or duty to disclose.

Confidential information acquired as a result of professional and business relationships must not be used for the personal advantage of the member or third parties.

Professional behaviour

A professional accountant should comply with relevant laws and regulations and should avoid any action that discredits the profession.

The importance of transparency and fairness

Transparency means openness (say, of discussions), clarity, lack of withholding of relevant information unless necessary.

Fairness means a sense of even-handedness and equality. Acting fairly is an ability to reach an equitable judgement in a given ethical situation.

chapter

8

Accounting for inventory

- Accounting for opening and closing inventory.
- Closing inventory reconciliation.
- Valuation of closing inventory.

Accounting for opening and closing inventory

At the beginning of the year

↓

Figure for inventory is always opening inventory

Purchases during year

↓

Always DEBIT purchases

↓

Never make an entry in inventory account

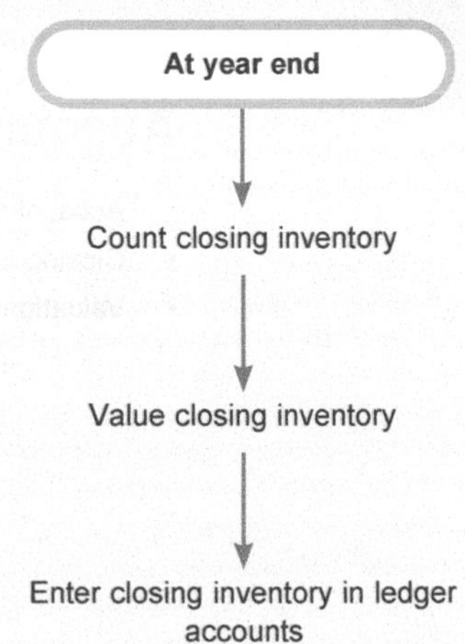

Trial balance

The trial balance will have a debit balance for opening inventory which is last year's closing inventory figure.

Inventory account

	£		£
Opening inventory	1,000		

Purchases during the year

Purchases during the year were £20,000.

Double entry:

Debit	Purchases account	£20,000
Credit	Bank/payables ledger control account	£20,000

No entry to the inventory account.

Year-end opening inventory and purchases

At end of the year, opening inventory account balance and purchases are cleared out to the statement of profit or loss:

Inventory account

	£		£
Opening inventory	1,000	Statement of profit or loss	1,000

Statement of profit or loss

	£	£
Sales (assumed figure)		35,000
Cost of sales		
Opening inventory	1,000	
Purchases	20,000	
	21,000	

Year-end closing inventory

Closing inventory at the year-end is valued at £2,000.

Enter closing inventory in inventory account

Double entry

Debit	Inventory account – Statement of financial position (asset)	£2,000
Credit	Closing inventory – Statement of profit or loss	£2,000

Inventory account

	£		£
Opening inventory	1,000	Statement of profit or loss	1,000

Closing Inventory – SFP

	£		£
Closing inventory SPL	2,000		

Closing Inventory – SPL

			£
Statement of profit or loss	2,000	Closing inventory SFP	2,000

Statement of profit or loss

	£	£
Sales/Revenue		35,000
Cost of sales		
Opening inventory	1,000	
Purchases	20,000	
	21,000	
Less: closing inventory	(2,000)	
Cost of sales		(19,000)
Gross profit		16,000

Balance on closing inventory account remains in account as opening inventory for the following year.

Inventory account

	£		£
Balance b/d	2,000		

CBA focus

Carrying forward closing inventory rather than charging against profit for the year is an example of the accruals/matching concept. When the inventory is sold in the following year, it will form part of cost of sales as the opening inventory. So the cost is matched with the revenue earned from selling the inventory.

Closing inventory reconciliation

Closing Inventory Valuation

↓

Count inventory items

↓

Reconcile inventory count to stores records

↓

Value inventory

Accounting software automates the process of recording, tracking and valuing inventory.

Stores records

- each line of inventory will have a bin card/inventory card
- shows quantity received from suppliers, issued for production/sale, returned to stores
- also shows quantity that should be on hand.

Reconciliation

Bin card balance

Possible reasons

- stores records not updated for delivery
- errors in stores records/counting.

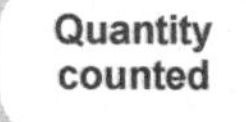

Bin card balance

Possible reasons

- stores records not updated for sale/ return to supplier
- errors in stores records/counting
- items stolen.

Valuation of closing inventory

IAS 2 rule

Inventory Valuation is the lower of

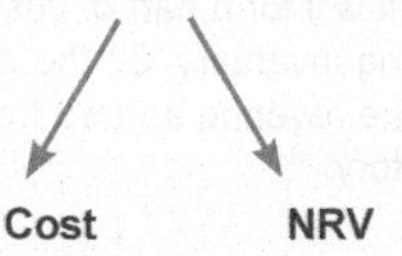

Cost **NRV**

- lower of cost and net realisable value
- rule applies to each individual line of inventory.

Cost = expenditure incurred in normal course of business in bringing product to present location and condition.

=
- purchase price
- import duties
- transport/handling costs
- direct production costs
- other overheads attributable to
- bringing product to present location and condition.

Net realisable value = sales proceeds expected from future sale after deducting any further costs to completion and selling costs.

Example

Closing inventory has been valued at £13,500; included in this are items which originally cost £2,000 but due to damage can only be sold for £1,500.

Solution

	£
Cost	2,000
NRV	(1,500)
Inventory adjustment required	500

Journal:

Debit Closing inventory – SPL	£500
Credit Closing inventory – SFP	£500

Final value for closing inventory in SPL and SFP = £13,500 – £500 = £13,000

CBA focus

In most examinations you will be required to put through an adjustment such as this for the closing inventory valuation.

CBA focus

Valuation of inventory at the lower of cost and NRV is an example of prudence in accounting. If it is likely that a loss will be made on the sale of the items (i.e. NRV < cost) then this should be recognised immediately by writing down the inventory at cost to NRV.

chapter

9

Irrecoverable and doubtful debts

- Irrecoverable and doubtful receivables.
- Accounting for irrecoverable debts.
- Accounting for doubtful receivables.
- Types of allowance for doubtful receivables.
- Recovery of debts.

Irrecoverable and doubtful receivables

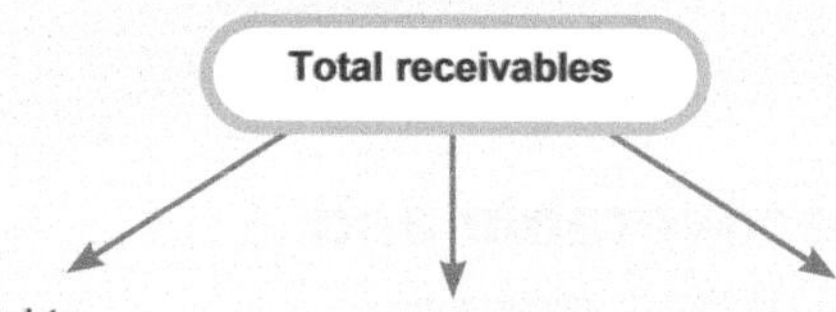

Irrecoverable debts (Bad debts)

- debts highly unlikely to be received
- written off

Doubtful receivables

- debts which may not be received
- allowance made and shown in statement of financial position

Good debts

- debts which are highly likely to be received
- shown as current asset in statement of financial position

Accounting for irrecoverable debts

- as irrecoverable debt is highly unlikely to be received it is written out of the books
- therefore removed from receivables (RLCA).

Double entry

Debit	Irrecoverable debts expense account (SPL)
Credit	Receivables ledger control account (SFP)

Example

Business has total receivables of £10,000 but one customer owing £600 has gone into liquidation and it is unlikely any money will be received.

Solution

Receivables ledger control account

	£		£
Balance b/d	10,000	Irrecoverable debts expense	600
		Balance c/d	9,400
	10,000		10,000
Balance b/d	9,400		

Irrecoverable debts expense account

	£		£
Receivables ledger control account	600	Statement of profit or loss	600
	600		600

Statement of financial position – receivables appear as £9,400.

Statement of profit or loss – expense for irrecoverable debts of £600.

Accounting for doubtful receivables

- doubtful receivables not as clear-cut as irrecoverable debt
- might be received but might not
- it is prudent to reflect this in final accounts.

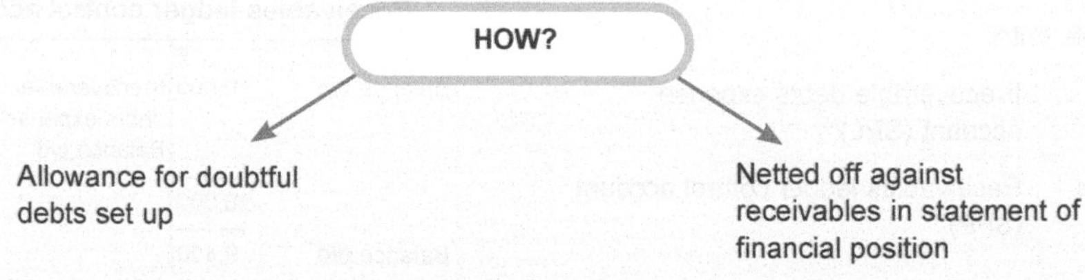

Double entry

Debit Allowance for doubtful receivables adjustment (SPL)

Credit Allowance for doubtful receivables account (SFP)

e.g

Example

At end of first year of trading, a business has total receivables of £20,000 and it is decided that of this amount £1,000 is doubtful.

Solution

Receivables ledger control account

	£		£
Balance b/d	20,000		

Allowance for doubtful receivables account

	£		£
		Allowance for doubtful receivables adjustment	1,000

Allowance for doubtful receivables adjustment account

	£		£
Allowance for doubtful receivables	1,000		

Statement of financial position – receivables shown as:

	£
Receivables	20,000
Less: allowance for doubtful receivables	(1,000)
	19,000

Statement of profit or loss account – expense for £1,000 for setting up allowance.

Subsequent years

- once an allowance for doubtful receivables account has been set up, it remains in the ledger accounts as a credit balance (statement of financial position item)
- each year adjusted for any increase/ decrease required.

Year 2

At the end of year 2, receivables are £30,000 of which £1,200 are thought to be doubtful.

Solution

Step 1

Set up opening balance on allowance account (closing balance at end of previous year).

Allowance for doubtful receivables account

	£		£
		Balance b/d	1,000

Step 2

Calculate allowance required at end of current year. In this example given as £1,200.

Step 3

Enter closing balance equal to the required new allowance. The figure to balance this account will be written off to the allowance for doubtful receivables adjustment account.

Allowance for doubtful receivables account

	£		£
Balance c/d	1,200	Balance b/d	1,000
		Allowance for doubtful receivables adjustment account	200
	1,200		1,200
		Balance b/d	1,200

Allowance for doubtful receivables adjustment account

	£		£
Allowance for doubtful receivables	200		

Statement of financial position – receivables shown as:

	£
Receivables	30,000
Less: Allowance for doubtful receivables	(1,200)
	28,800

Statement of profit or loss – expense for £200 for increasing allowance.

Year 3

At end of year 3, receivables total £21,000 of which £900 are thought to be doubtful.

Solution

Step 1

Set up opening balance on allowance account (closing balance at end of year 2).

Allowance for doubtful receivables account

	£		£
		Balance b/d	1,200

Step 2

Calculate allowance required at end of current year (in this example given as £900).

Step 3

Enter closing balance equal to the required new allowance (£900). The figure to balance the account will be written off to the allowance for doubtful receivables adjustment account – in this case a write back to profit.

Allowance for doubtful receivables account

	£		£
Allowance for doubtful receivables adjustment account	300	Balance b/d	1,200
Balance c/d	900		
	1,200		1,200
		Balance b/d	900

Allowance for doubtful receivables adjustment account

	£		£
		Allowance for doubtful receivables	300

Statement of financial position – receivables shown as:

	£
Receivables	21,000
Less: allowance for doubtful receivables	(900)
	20,100

Statement of profit or loss – credited with £300 for decreasing allowance.

CBA focus

In the examination you will always have to deal with adjustments for irrecoverable debts and doubtful receivables allowances. Remember that if there is already an allowance for doubtful receivables then only the increase or decrease to the allowance needs to be charged/credited to the statement of profit or loss.

Types of allowance for doubtful receivables

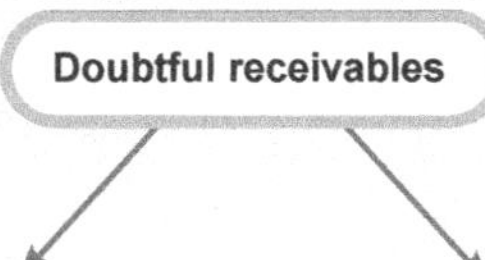

Specific allowance

- particular debt is identified as doubtful e.g. debt from Mr F

General allowance

- business experience indicates that a certain % of debts may not be paid e.g. 5%

Example

A business has a current allowance for doubtful receivables of £500. Total receivables at the year-end are £31,000. It is decided to make an allowance for one particular debt of £800 and to make a general allowance against 2% of remaining receivables.

Solution

Step 1

Set up opening balance on allowance account.

Allowance for doubtful receivables account

	£		£
		Balance b/d	500

Step 2

Calculate allowance required at end of current year.

	£
Specific allowance	800
General allowance	
(£31,000 – £800) x 2%	604
Total allowance required	1,404

Step 3

Enter closing balance equal to the required new allowance (£1,404). The figure to balance the account will be written off to the allowance for doubtful receivables adjustment account.

Allowance for doubtful receivables account

	£		£
Balance c/d	1,404	Balance b/d	500
		Allowance for doubtful debt adjustment account	904
	1,404		1,404
		Balance b/d	1,404

Allowance for doubtful receivables adjustment account

	£		£
Allowance for doubtful receivables	904		

Statement of financial position – receivables shown as

	£
Receivables	31,000
Less: allowance for doubtful receivables	1,404
	29,596

Statement of profit or loss – expense of £904 for increasing allowance.

CBA focus

Whether the allowance for doubtful receivables is a specific or general provision or a mixture of the two, there is no difference in the basic accounting.

Calculate the allowance required at the year-end and enter this as the balance c/d on the account. The amount to balance the account will be written off/back to statement of profit or loss.

Recovery of debts

Debt previously written off

- debt is written off in one year
- in a later year it is unexpectedly received.

Double entry

Debit	Cash/bank account
Credit	Irrecoverable debts expense account

Debt previously provided for

- debt has allowance made against it in one year
- in a later year it is unexpectedly received
- debt is still in RLCA as it has not been written off.

Double entry

Debit	Cash/bank account
Credit	Receivables ledger control account

chapter

10

Control account reconciliations

- Types of reconciliation.
- Receivables ledger control account.
- Payables ledger control account.
- Receivables ledger control account reconciliation.
- Payables ledger control account reconciliation.

Types of reconciliation

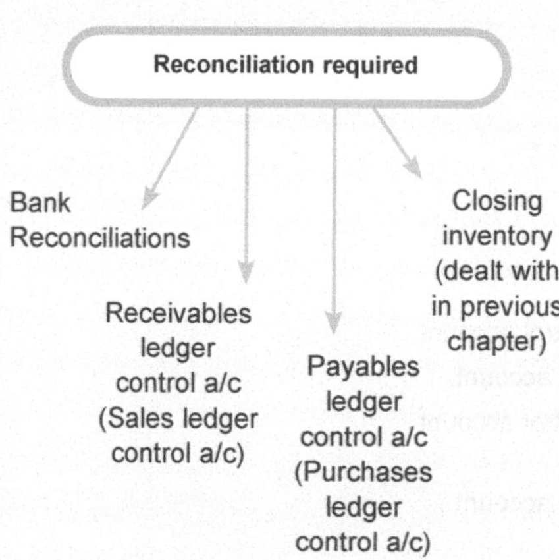

Receivables ledger control account

(also known as sales ledger control account)
Typical receivables ledger control account:

Receivables ledger control account

	Note	£		Note	£
Balance b/d	(i)	3,400	SRDB	(iii)	1,800
SDB	(ii)	20,600	CRB – cash	(iv)	19.500
			Discounts allowed	(v)	1,200
			Irrecoverable debt write-off	(vi)	400
			Contra	(vii)	200
			Balance c/d		900
		24,000			24,000
Balance b/d		900			

Notes

(i) Opening balance = asset = debit balance

(ii) Sales invoices posted from sales day book

(iii) Credit notes posted from sales returns day book

(iv) Cash receipts posted from cash receipts book

(v) Discounts allowed posted from discounts allowed book

(vi) Irrecoverable debt written off (see earlier chapter)

(vii) Contra entry with payables ledger control account.

e.g

Example

Contra entry

- a customer who owes us £200 is also a supplier and we owe him £300. It has been agreed that the two amounts should be set off by a contra entry, leaving only £100 owed by us to the supplier.

Solution

Double entry:

Debit Payables ledger control account	£200
Credit Receivables ledger control account	£200

Payables ledger control account (also known as purchases ledger control account)

Typical payables ledger control account:

Payables ledger control account

	Note	£		Note	£
PRDB	(iii)	900	Balance b/d	(i)	2,100
CPB – cash	(iv)	13,300	PDB	(ii)	15,800
Discounts received	(v)	700			
Contra entry	(vi)	200			
Balance c/d		2,800			
		17,900			17,900
			Balance b/d		2,800

Notes

(i) Opening balance = liability = credit balance

(ii) Purchases invoices posted from purchases day book

(iii) Credit notes posted from purchases returns day book

(iv) Cash paid to suppliers posted from cash payments book

(v) Discounts received posted from discounts received book

(vi) Contra entry (see above).

Receivables ledger control account reconciliation

- the receivables ledger control account is written up using totals from sales day book, sales returns day book, discounts allowed book and cash receipts book.
- individual accounts for receivables in the subsidiary receivables ledger are written up using the individual entries from the sales day book, sales returns day book, discounts allowed book and cash receipts book.
- as both are written up from the same sources of information, at the end of the period the balance on the receivables ledger control account should equal the total of the list of balances in the subsidiary receivables ledger.

RLCA balance = **Total of list of subsidiary receivables ledger balances**

Purpose of receivables ledger control account reconciliation

- to show that the balance in the RLCA does in fact equal the total of the list of balances
- to indicate that there are errors in either the RLCA or the subsidiary receivables ledger accounts if the two are not equal
- to find the correct figure for total receivables to appear in the trial balance.

Preparing a receivables ledger control account reconciliation.

Step 1

- extract list of balances from the subsidiary receivables ledger

Step 2

- balance the receivables ledger control account.

Step 3

- If the two figures are different, the reasons for the difference must be investigated.

Step 4

- correct any errors that affect the receivables ledger control account
- find corrected balance on the receivables ledger control account.

Step 5

- correct any errors that affect the total of the list of balances from the subsidiary receivables ledger
- find corrected total of list of subsidiary receivables ledger balances.

Example

Receivables ledger control account reconciliation

The balance on the receivables ledger control account at 31 May is £4,100. The individual balances on the subsidiary receivables ledger are as follows:

	£
receivable A	1,200
receivable B	300
receivable C	2,000
receivable D	1,000

Step 1

Extract list of balances from the subsidiary receivables ledger accounts and total.

	£
receivable A	1,200
receivable B	300
receivable C	2,000
receivable D	1,000
	4,500

Step 2

- Balance the receivables ledger control account.

The balance has been given as £4,100.

Step 3

- If the two figures are different, the reasons for the difference must be investigated.

You are given the following information:

- a page of the sales day book had been undercast by £100
- a credit note for £50 to Receivable A had been entered into A's subsidiary receivables ledger account as an invoice
- a contra entry with Receivable B for £200 had only been entered in the receivables ledger control account not the individual subsidiary receivables ledger account.

Step 4

- correct any errors that affect the receivables ledger control account
- Find corrected balance on receivables ledger control account.

Receivables ledger control account

	£		£
Original balance	4,100	Corrected balance	4,200
SDB undercast	100		
	4,200		4,200
Corrected balance	4,200		

If the sales day book was undercast, then the amount posted to the receivables ledger control account was £100 too small and therefore an additional debit entry for £100 is needed in the control account.

The other two adjustments affect the individual accounts not the control account.

Step 5

- correct any errors that affect the total of the list of balances from the subsidiary receivables ledger

- Find corrected total of list of receivables ledger balances.

	£
Subsidiary receivables ledger account	
list total	4,500
Less:	
Credit note entered as invoice	(100)
Less: Contra	(200)
Corrected list of balances	4,200

As the credit note for £50 had been entered as an invoice instead, the list of balances must be reduced by £100 to reflect the removal of the invoice and the entry of the credit note.

The contra had only been entered in the receivables ledger control account and therefore the same £200 must be deducted from the list of balances.

Credit balances on receivables ledger accounts

- normally a receivables balance on the subsidiary receivables ledger account will be a debit balance brought down (asset balance – money owed from receivable)
- sometimes, however, the balance will be a credit balance.

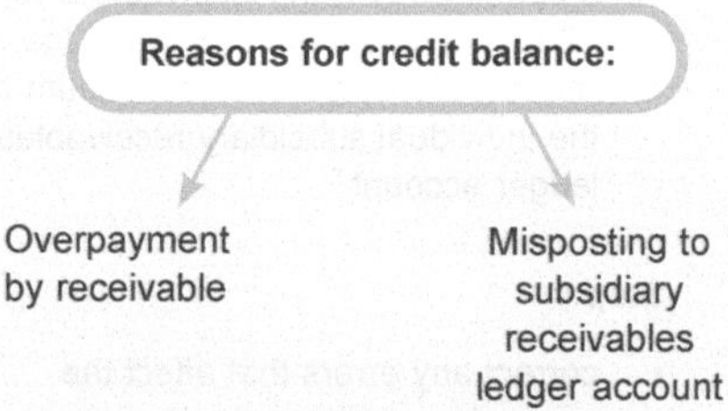

Reasons for credit balance:

- Overpayment by receivable
- Misposting to subsidiary receivables ledger account

Treatment of credit balance

- when the list of receivables ledger balances is drawn up and totalled, the credit balance must be deducted rather than added.

Payables ledger control account reconciliation

- the payables ledger control account is written up using totals from purchases day book, purchases returns day book, discounts received book and cash payments book
- individual accounts for payables in the subsidiary payables ledger are written up using the individual entries from the purchases day book, purchases returns day book, discounts received book and cash payments book
- as both are written up from the same sources of information, then at the end of the period the balance on the payables ledger control account should equal the total of the list of balances in the subsidiary payables ledger

PLCA balance = **Total of list of subsidiary payables ledger balances**

Purpose of payables ledger control account reconciliation

- to show that PLCA does in fact equal the total of the list of balances
- to indicate that there are errors in either the PLCA or the subsidiary payables ledger accounts if the two are not equal
- to find the correct figure for total payables to appear in the trial balance.

Preparing a payables ledger control account reconciliation

Step 1

- extract list of balances from subsidiary payables ledger accounts and total.

Step 2

- balance the payables ledger control account.

Step 3

- if the two figures are different the reasons for the difference must be investigated.

Step 4

- correct any errors that affect the payables ledger control account
- find corrected balance on payables ledger control account.

Step 5

- correct any errors that affect the total of the list of balances from the subsidiary payables ledger
- find corrected total of list of subsidiary payables ledger balances.

Example

Payables ledger control account reconciliation

The balance on the payables ledger control account at 31May is £2,000.The individual balances on the subsidiary payables ledger are as follows:

	£
payable E	800
payable F	600
payable G	400
payable H	700

Step 1

- Extract list of balances from subsidiary payables ledger accounts and total.

	£
payable E	800
payable F	600
payable G	400
payable H	700
	2,500

Step 2

- Balance the payables ledger control account.

The balance has been given as £2,000.

Step 3

- If the two figures are different, the reasons for the difference must be investigated.

You are given the following information:

- a page of the purchases returns day book had been overcast by £1,000
- discounts received from suppliers totalling £680 had not been posted to the control account
- an invoice from payable G for £350 had been entered into the individual account in the payables ledger as £530.

Step 4

- correct any errors that affect the payables ledger control account
- find corrected balance on payables ledger control account.

Payables ledger control account

	£		£
Discounts received	680	Original balance	2,000
Corrected balance	2,320	PRDB overcast	1,000
	3,000		3,000
		Corrected balance	2,320

If the purchases returns day book was overcast, then the amount posted to the payables ledger control account on the debit side for returns was £1,000 too big and therefore an additional credit entry for £1,000 is needed in the control account.

The discounts received of £680 were omitted from the control account and therefore the control account must be debited with this amount.

Step 5

- correct any errors that affect the total of the list of balances from the subsidiary payables ledger
- find corrected total of list of balances.

	£
Subsidiary payables ledger account list total	2,500
Less: 'transposition error' on invoice (530 – 350)	(180)
Corrected list of balances	2,320

The invoice had been entered as £180 higher than it should have been and therefore the total of the list of balances must reduced by £180.

Debit balances on payables ledger accounts

- normally a payable's balance on his subsidiary payables ledger account will be a credit balance brought down (liability – money owed to payable)
- sometimes, however, the balance will be a debit balance.

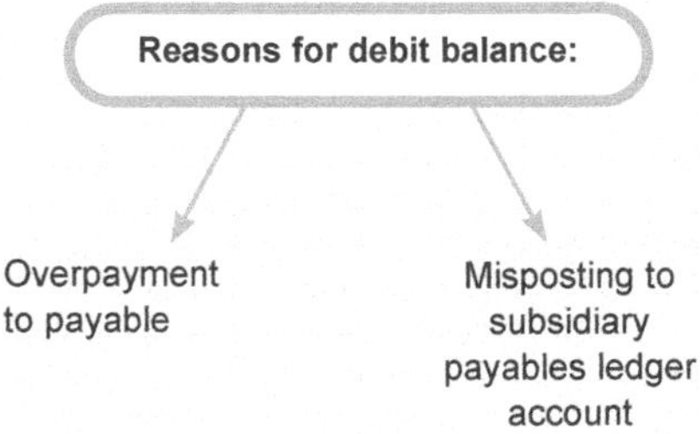

Reasons for debit balance:

Overpayment to payable

Misposting to subsidiary payables ledger account

Treatment of debit balance

- when the list of subsidiary payables ledger balances is drawn up and totalled, the debit balance must be deducted rather than added.

chapter

11

Bank reconciliations

- Bank control account reconciliation.

Bank control account reconciliation

At regular intervals the cashier must check that the cash book is correct by comparing the cash book with the bank statement.

Why might they not agree?

Cheques we've paid in have not yet been cleared = "uncleared lodgements" (Bank statement not fully up to date – our records fine).

Cheques we have written have not yet been taken to bank by the recipients or have not yet cleared = "unpresented cheques" (Bank statement not fully up to date – our records fine).

Bank Charges / Interest we haven't accounted for (need to update our records for these).

Example

The following differences have been identified when comparing the cash book with the bank statements.

(i) Bank interest received £80, had not been entered in the cashbook
(ii) A BACS receipt of £12,400 and £920 from two customers has not been entered in the cashbook
(iii) A receipt for £1,300 has been recorded in the cashbook as £1,500
(iv) Cheques drawn for £7,880 entered in the cashbook are not showing on the bank statement.

Using the table below show those items that would be required to update the cashbook.

Adjustment	Amount £	Debit	Credit
(i)	80	✓	
(ii)	13,320	✓	
(iii)	200		✓

chapter

12

Accruals and prepayments

- Accruals concept.
- Accrued expenses.
- Prepaid expenses.
- Accrued and prepaid income.

Accruals concept

Accruals concept

Income/expenses dealt with in statement of profit or loss in period in which earned/incurred not period in which cash received/paid

Accrued expenses

An accrued expense is an expense incurred but not yet paid for. In accordance with the accruals concept the expense and a corresponding liability should be recognised.

Example

A business has a year end of 31 December. On 1 May 20X5 a new building was rented with quarterly rentals in arrears of £1,500.

Payments for the year ended 31 December 20X5 were:

Date	Quarter ended	£
31 July	31 July X5	1,500
31 Oct	31 Oct X5	1,500

What is the accrual for rent at 31 December 20X5?

Solution

£3,000 is recorded in the rent account as an expense (the cash paid):

Rent expenses

		£		£
31 July X5	Bank	1,500		
31 Oct X5	Bank	1,500		

However, the building has been occupied during November and December even though the rent has not yet been paid. This must be accrued:

Accrual = £1,500 x 2/3

= £1,000

Accounting entry for accrued expense:

Dr Rent expenses (SPL)
Cr Accrued expenses (SFP)

The debit entry increases the expense recognised in the rent expenses account within the SPL.

The credit entry recognises a liability in the SFP.

Statement of profit or loss – charge of £4,000 (8 months @ £500 per month)

Statement of financial position – accrual of £1,000 in current liabilities

Continuing the previous example, the business continues to rent the building during 20X6.

Payments of rent are as follows:

Date	Quarter ended	£
31 Jan	31 Jan X6	1,500
30 Apr	30 Apr X6	1,500
31 July	31 July X6	1,800
31 Oct	31 Oct X6	1,800

Write up the ledger account for year ended 31 December 20X6.

Solution

Step 1

Enter the reversal of the opening accrued expense as a credit balance (£1,500 x 2/3 months).

Rent expenses

	£		£
		1 Jan X6 Reversal of accrued expenses	1,000

Step 2

Enter payments for the year:

Rent expenses

	£		£
31 Jan X6 Bank	1,500	1 Jan X6 Reversal of accrued expenses	1,000
30 Apr X6 Bank	1,500		
31 July X6 Bank	1,800		
31 Oct X6 Bank	1,800		

Step 3

Calculate the closing accrual (November and December rent not yet paid):

Accrual = £1,800 x 2/3 months
= £1,200

Step 4

Enter closing accrual in the rent account and balance the account to find the rent charge for the year to 31 December 20X6:

Rent account

	£		£
31 Jan X6 Bank	1,500	1 Jan X6 Reversal of accrued expenses	1,000
30 Apr X6 Bank	1,500		
31 July X6 Bank	1,800	31 Dec X6	
31 Oct X6 Bank	1,800	Expense for the year	6,800
31 Dec X6 Accrued expenses	1,200		
	7,800		7,800
		1 Jan X7 Reversal of accrued expenses	1,200

Proof of SPL charge

	£
Jan X6 to April X6 (4 months @ £500 per month)	2,000
May X6 to Dec X6 (8 months @ £600 per month)	4,800
Total rent expense	6,800

Prepaid expenses

A prepaid expense is an expense already paid for although it has not yet been incurred so that an asset should be recognised.

Example

1 April 20X5 insurance policy for £6,000 taken out payable for next 12-month period. Business has 31 December year-end. Write up the ledger account for the year to 31 December 20X5.

Solution

Year to 31 December 20X5:

Insurance account

	£		£
1 Apr X5 Bank	6,000		

At 31 December 20X5 insurance has already been paid for January to March 20X6:

Prepayment = £6,000 x 3/12
= £1,500

Accounting entry for prepaid expense:

Dr Prepaid expenses (SFP)
Cr Insurance expenses (SPL)

The credit entry decreases the expense recognised in the insurance expenses account within the SPL as although it was paid for it does not relate to this accounting period.

The debit entry recognises an asset in the SFP.

Insurance account

	£		£
1 Apr X5 Bank	6,000	31 Dec X5 Expense for year	4,500
		31 Dec X5 Prepaid expenses	1,500
	6,000		6,000

SPL charge = £4,500 (9 months' insurance @ £500 per month)

SFP = £1,500 prepayment (debit balance brought down on insurance account) shown in current assets

Continuing the example, the insurance payment on 1 April 20X6 increases to £8,400.

First the reversal of the opening prepaid expense as a debit balance must be made.

Solution

Insurance account

	£		£
1 Jan X6 Reversal of prepaid expenses	1,500	31 Dec X6 Expense for the year	7,800
1 Apr X6 Bank	8,400	31 Dec X6 Prepaid expenses (8,400x3/12)	2,100
	9,900		9,900
1 Jan X7 Reversal of prepaid expense	2,100		

Proof of SPL charge

	£
Jan X6 to March X6 – 3 months @ £500 per month	1,500
April X6 to December X6 – 9 months @ £700 per month	6,300
Total SPL charge	7,800

CBA focus

In the examination you will have to deal with accruals and prepayments in many different contexts such as adjusting a trial balance figure and putting adjustments onto an extended trial balance. However, in many examinations you will also be required to complete an expense account showing opening and closing accruals or prepayments and the statement of profit or loss charge for the period.

Opening accruals and prepayments are the reversal of the prior accounting period's closing accruals and prepayments.

Accrued and prepaid income

- e.g. rent received
- income credited to SPL is amount earned in period not cash received

Cash received>income earned =income prepaid

Cash received<income earned =income accrued

Example

Business has two properties which it rents out.

Property A	Rental £8,000 per annum Cash received £10,000
Property B	Rental £6,000 per annum Cash received £5,000

Solution

Rental income – property A

	£		£
Income for the year	8,000	Cash	10,000
Prepaid income	2,000		
	10,000		10,000
		Reversal of prepaid income	2,000

Rental income – property B

	£		£
Income for the year	6,000	Cash	5,000
		Accrued income	1,000
	6,000		6,000
Reversal of accrued income	1,000		

Statement of financial position

	£
Current asset	
Accrued income	1,000
Current liabilities	
Income prepaid	2,000

chapter

13

Suspense accounts and errors

- What is a trial balance?
- Errors.
- Journal entries.
- Suspense account.
- Correcting errors.
- Errors and the suspense account.
- Clearing the suspense account.

What is a trial balance?

- a list of all of the ledger balances in the general ledger
- debit and credit balances are listed separately
- debit balance total should equal credit balance total.

Illustration – trial balance

	Debit balances £	Credit balances £
Sales		5,000
Wages	100	
Purchases	3,000	
Rent	200	
Car	3,000	
RLCA	100	
PLCA		1,400
	6,400	6,400

Errors

In a manual accounting system, errors will be made – some are identified by extracting a trial balance but others will not be.

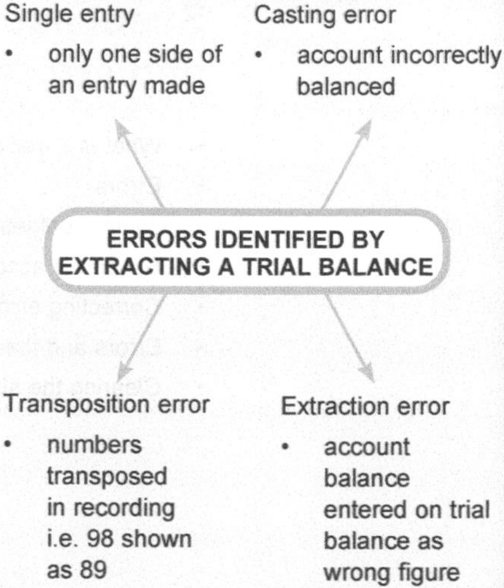

ERRORS IDENTIFIED BY EXTRACTING A TRIAL BALANCE

Single entry
- only one side of an entry made

Casting error
- account incorrectly balanced

Transposition error
- numbers transposed in recording i.e. 98 shown as 89

Extraction error
- account balance entered on trial balance as wrong figure

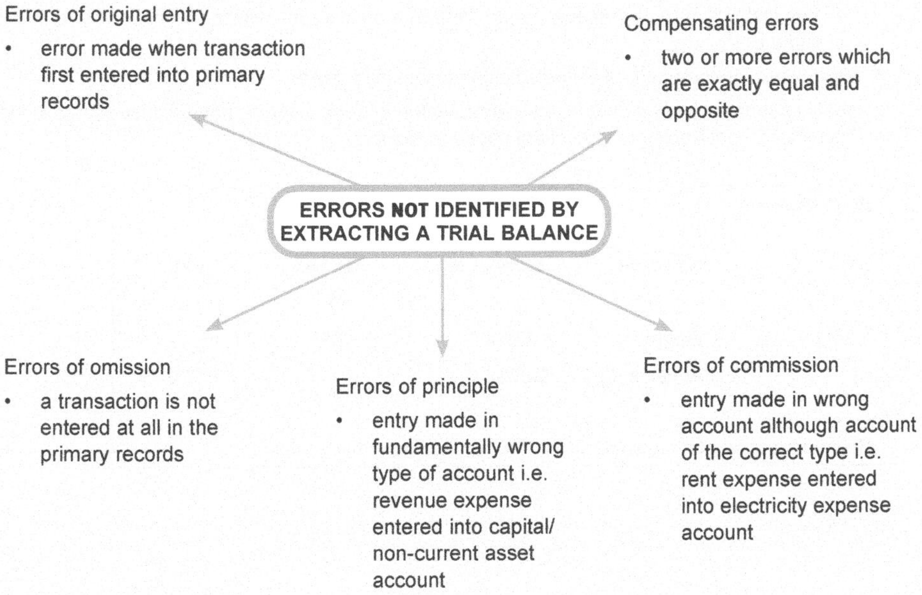

ERRORS NOT IDENTIFIED BY EXTRACTING A TRIAL BALANCE

Errors of original entry

- error made when transaction first entered into primary records

Compensating errors

- two or more errors which are exactly equal and opposite

Errors of omission

- a transaction is not entered at all in the primary records

Errors of principle

- entry made in fundamentally wrong type of account i.e. revenue expense entered into capital/ non-current asset account

Errors of commission

- entry made in wrong account although account of the correct type i.e. rent expense entered into electricity expense account

Journal entries

- written instruction to bookkeeper to put through a double entry which has not come from books of prime entry
- also used for correction of errors/adjustments/unusual items
- only used for adjusting double entry errors in the general ledger – not used for entries in the subsidiary receivables or subsidiary payables ledgers.

Journal format

Date	Narrative	Account ref	Debit	Credit
			£	£
1 May	Electricity	GL014	200	
	Advertising	GL022		200

Being correction of misposting of electricity bill to advertising account

Suspense account

Bookkeeper does not know what to do with one side of an entry and therefore posts it to a suspense account.

Example

£200 received but bookkeeper does not know what it is for so debits cash receipts book and credits suspense account.

When trial balance totals disagree used to balance the trial balance temporarily.

Example

Total of debit balances on trial balance is £35,000 but total of credit balances is £34,000. £1,000 credited to suspense account to make trial balance equal.

Correcting errors

- errors corrected by putting through a journal for the correcting entry.

How to find correcting entry

- work out the double entry that has been done
- work out the double entry that should have been done
- draft journal entry to go from what has been done to what should have been done.

Example

Journal entries

(i) An amount of £200 of electricity bill payments was entered into the advertising account.

What has been done?

Debit	Advertising account	£200
Credit	Bank account	£200

What should have been done?

Debit	Electricity account	£200
Credit	Bank account	£200

Journal entry

Debit	Electricity account	£200
Credit	Advertising account	£200

(ii) A purchase invoice for £1,000 had not been entered into the books of prime entry (ignore VAT).

What has been done?

No entries at all

What should have been done?

Debit	Purchases account	£1,000
Credit	PLCA	£1,000

Journal entry

Debit	Purchases account	£1,000
Credit	PLCA	£1,000

(iii) An irrecoverable debt for £100 is to be written off.

This is not correction of an error but an adjustment to be made.

Journal entry

Debit	Irrecoverable debts expense account	£100
Credit	RLCA	£100

(iv) A contra entry for £500 has been entered in the general ledger control accounts but has not been entered in the subsidiary payables ledger.

No journal entry is required as the error is not in the general ledger but the subsidiary ledger. However, the payables account in the subsidiary payables ledger must be debited to reflect this contra entry.

CBA focus

In most examinations you will be required to draft journal entries to correct errors.

Errors and the suspense account

Some errors made will affect the trial balance and therefore are effectively part of the suspense account balance.

Example

(i) Discounts allowed of £150 have been entered as a credit entry in the discounts allowed account.

What has been done?

Credit Discounts allowed account	£150
Credit Receivables ledger control account	£150

What should have been done?

Debit Discounts allowed account	£150
Credit Receivables ledger control account	£150

Journal

Debit Discounts allowed account	£300
Credit Suspense account	£300

The discounts allowed account has been credited rather than debited with £150; therefore, to turn this into a debit of £150, it needs to be debited with £300. No other account is incorrect so the other side of the entry is to the suspense account.

(ii) The balance for motor expenses of £400 has been omitted from the trial balance.

What has been done?

The motor expenses balance of £400 has been omitted from the trial balance.

What should be done?

A £400 debit balance (expense) must appear on the trial balance.

Journal

Debit	Motor expenses (TB)	£400
Credit	Suspense account	£400

Clearing the suspense account

The suspense account cannot remain as a permanent account and must eventually be investigated and cleared.

Example

A business has a suspense account with a debit balance of £80.

The following errors were noted:

(i) rent of £750 was entered into the rent account as £570

(ii) an advertising bill was overstated in the advertising account by £100

Journals

(i) Debit	Rent account	£180
Credit	Suspense account	£180
(ii) Debit	Suspense account	£100
Credit	Advertising account	£100

Suspense account

	£		£
Opening balance	80	Rent	180
Advertising	100		
	180		180

The suspense account is now cleared.

CBA focus

In most examinations you will be required to draft journal entries to clear a suspense account balance or to put adjustments through an extended trial balance in order to clear the suspense account.

chapter

14

Extended trial balance – in action

- Preparing an extended trial balance.

Preparing an extended trial balance

Step 1

Enter each ledger name and balance in trial balance columns.

Step 2

Total initial trial balance columns to ensure they are equal or set up a suspense account.

Step 3

Put through adjustments/amend errors in adjustments columns.

Step 4

Total adjustments columns to ensure double entry correct.

Step 5

Cross-cast each account line and enter total in either SPL or SFP columns.

Step 6

Total SPL a/c columns

– difference will be the profit/loss to be entered in SFP column as well.

Step 7

Total SFP columns.

e.g

Example

Initial trial balance of a sole trader at 30 June 20X6

	£	£
Sales		40,000
Purchases	20,000	
Inventory at 1 July 20X5	2,000	
Non-current assets at cost	40,000	
Accumulated depreciation at 1 July 20X5		18,000
Receivables ledger control account	4,400	
Bank	1,000	
Payables ledger control		2,500
Drawings	10,000	
Capital		28,100
Rent	2,400	
Wages	5,600	
Heat and light	3,200	
	88,600	88,600

The following points are also noted:

(i) Depreciation charge at 15% straight-line is to be provided for the year

(ii) There is an accrual for electricity of £300

(iii) There is a prepayment of rent of £500

(iv) An irrecoverable debt of £400 is to be written off

(v) An allowance of 5% of remaining receivables is to be set up for doubtful receivables

(vi) Closing inventory has been valued at £2,200.

Solution

Step 1
Enter each ledger name and balance in trial balance columns.

Account name	Trial balance		Adjustments		Statement of profit or loss		Statement of financial position	
	DR	CR	DR	CR	DR	CR	DR	CR
	£	£	£	£	£	£	£	£
Sales		40,000						
Purchases	20,000							
Inventory at 1 July 20X5	2,000							
Non-current assets at cost	40,000							
Accumulated depreciation at 1 July 20X5		18,000						
Receivables ledger control	4,400							
Bank	1,000							
Payables ledger control		2,500						
Drawings	10,000							
Capital		28,100						
Rent	2,400							
Wages	5,600							
Heat and light	3,200							

Step 3

Put through adjustments/amend errors in adjustments columns.

We will firstly draft journal entries for each adjustment then enter them into the ETB.

(i) Depreciation charge at 15% straight-line is to be provided for the year

Depreciation charge = £40,000 x 15%

= £6,000

Journal

Debit	Depreciation charge	£6,000
Credit	Accumulated depreciation	£6,000

As there is no depreciation charge account, this must be set up when entered onto the ETB.

(ii) There is an accrual for electricity of £300

Journal

Debit	Heat and Light	£300
Credit	Accruals	£300

Accruals account must be set up on ETB

(iii) There is a prepayment of rent of £500

Journal

Debit	Prepayments	£500
Credit	Rent	£500

Prepayments account must be set up on ETB.

(iv) An irrecoverable debt of £400 is to be written off.

Journal

Debit Irrecoverable debts expense £400

Credit Receivables ledger control £400

Irrecoverable expense account must be set up on ETB

(v) An allowance of 5% of remaining receivables is to be set up for doubtful receivables.

Amount of allowance = (£4,400 – £400) x 5%

= £200

Journal

Debit Allowance for doubtful receivables adjustment £200

Credit Allowance for doubtful receivables £200

Allowance for doubtful receivables account must be set up on ETB

(vi) Closing inventory has been valued at £2,200.

Debit Inventory account – SFP £2,200

Credit Inventory account – SPL £2,200

Both of these accounts must be set up on the ETB.

Account name	Trial balance		Adjustments		Statement of profit or loss		Statement of financial position	
	DR £	CR £	DR £	CR £	DR £	CR £	DR £	CR £
Sales		40,000						
Purchases	20,000							
Inventory at 1 July 20X5	2,000							
Non-current assets at cost	40,000							
Accumulated depreciation at 1 July 20X5		18,000		6,000				
Receivables ledger control	4,400			400				
Bank	1,000							
Payables ledger control		2,500						
Drawings	10,000							
Capital		28,100						
Rent	2,400			500				
Wages	5,600							
Heat and light	3,200		300					
Depreciation charge			6,000					
Accruals				300				
Prepayments			500					
Irrecoverable debts expense			400					
Allowance for doubtful receivables adjustment			200					
Allowance for doubtful receivables				200				
Inventory – SFP			2,200					
Inventory – SPL				2,200				
	88,600	88,600						

Step 4: Total adjustments columns to ensure double entry correct. Make sure that you leave a spare line at the bottom for the net profit/loss figure in step 6.

Account name	Trial balance		Adjustments		Statement of profit or loss		Statement of financial position	
	DR £	CR £	DR £	CR £	DR £	CR £	DR £	CR £
Sales		40,000						
Purchases	20,000							
Inventory at 1 July 20X5	2,000							
Non-current assets at cost	40,000							
Accumulated depreciation at 1 July 20X5		18,000		6,000				
Receivables ledger control	4,400			400				
Bank	1,000							
Payables ledger control		2,500						
Drawings	10,000							
Capital		28,100						
Rent	2,400			500				
Wages	5,600							
Heat and light	3,200		300					
Depreciation charge			6,000					
Accruals				300				
Prepayments			500					
Irrecoverable debts expense			400					
Allowance for doubtful receivables adjustment			200					
Allowance for doubtful receivables				200				
Inventory – SFP			2,200					
Inventory – SPL				2,200				
	88,600	88,600	9,600	9,600				

Step 5

Cross-cast each account line and enter total in either SPL a/c or SFP column.

Income/expense accounts are entered in the SPL a/c columns.

Asset/liability accounts are entered in the SFP columns.

CBA focus

Take care with drawings as these are a statement of financial position item, being a reduction in capital.

Account name	Trial balance		Adjustments		Statement of profit or loss		Statement of financial position	
	DR	CR	DR	CR	DR	CR	DR	CR
	£	£	£	£	£	£	£	£
Sales		40,000				40,000		
Purchases	20,000				20,000			
Inventory at 1 July 20X5	2,000				2,000			
Non-current assets at cost	40,000						40,000	
Accumulated depreciation at 1 July 20X5		18,000		6,000				24,000
Receivables ledger control	4,400			400			4,000	
Bank	1,000						1,000	
Payables ledger control		2,500						2,500
Drawings	10,000						10,000	
Capital		28,100						28,100
Rent	2,400			500	1,900			
Wages	5,600				5,600			
Heat and light	3,200		300		3,500			
Depreciation charge			6,000		6,000			
Accruals				300				300
Prepayments			500				500	
Irrecoverable debts expense			400		400			
Allowance for doubtful receivables adjustment			200		200			
Allowance for doubtful receivables				200				200
Inventory – SFP			2,200				2,200	
Inventory – SPL				2,200		2,200		
	88,600	88,600	9,600	9,600				

Step 6

Total SPL a/c columns – the difference will be profit/loss to be entered in SFP column as well.

When the difference is found between the two IS column totals, this must be entered to make the two columns equal.

Debit entry = Profit = Credit entry in SFP

Credit entry = Loss = Debit entry in SFP

Step 7

Total SFP columns.

Step 6

Account name	Trial balance		Adjustments		Statement of profit or loss		Statement of financial position	
	DR	CR	DR	CR	DR	CR	DR	CR
	£	£	£	£	£	£	£	£
Sales		40,000				40,000		
Purchases	20,000				20,000			
Inventory at 1 July 20X5	2,000				2,000			
Non-current assets at cost	40,000						40,000	
Accumulated depreciation at 1 July 20X5		18,000		6,000				24,000
Receivables ledger control	4,400			400			4,000	
Bank	1,000						1,000	
Payables ledger control		2,500						2,500
Drawings	10,000						10,000	
Capital		28,100						28,100
Rent	2,400			500	1,900			
Wages	5,600				5,600			
Heat and light	3,200		300		3,500			
Depreciation charge			6,000		6,000			
Accruals				300				300
Prepayments			500				500	
Irrecoverable debts expense			400		400			
Allowance for doubtful receivables adjustment			200		200			
Allowance for doubtful receivables				200				200
Inventory – SFP			2,200				2,200	
Inventory – SPL				2,200		2,200		
Net profit					2,600			2,600
	88,600	88,600	9,600	9,600	42,200	42,200		

Step 7

Account name	Trial balance		Adjustments		Statement of profit or loss		Statement of financial position	
	DR £	CR £	DR £	CR £	DR £	CR £	DR £	CR £
Sales		40,000				40,000		
Purchases	20,000				20,000			
Inventory at 1 July 20X5	2,000				2,000			
Non-current assets at cost	40,000						40,000	
Accumulated depreciation at 1 July 20X5		18,000		6,000				24,000
Receivables ledger control	4,400			400			4,000	
Bank	1,000						1,000	
Payables ledger control		2,500						2,500
Drawings	10,000						10,000	
Capital		28,100						28,100
Rent	2,400			500	1,900			
Wages	5,600				5,600			
Heat and light	3,200		300		3,500			
Depreciation charge			6,000		6,000			
Accruals				300				300
Prepayments			500				500	
Irrecoverable debts expense			400		400			
Allowance for doubtful receivables adjustment			200		200			
Allowance for doubtful receivables				200				200
Inventory – SFP			2,200				2,200	
Inventory – SPL				2,200		2,200		
Net profit					2,600			2,600
	88,600	88,600	9,600	9,600	42,200	42,200	57,700	57,700

chapter

15

Sole trader accounts

- Closing off ledger accounts.
- Drawings.
- Preparing final accounts from an extended trial balance.
- Preparing final accounts from an initial trial balance.

Closing off ledger accounts

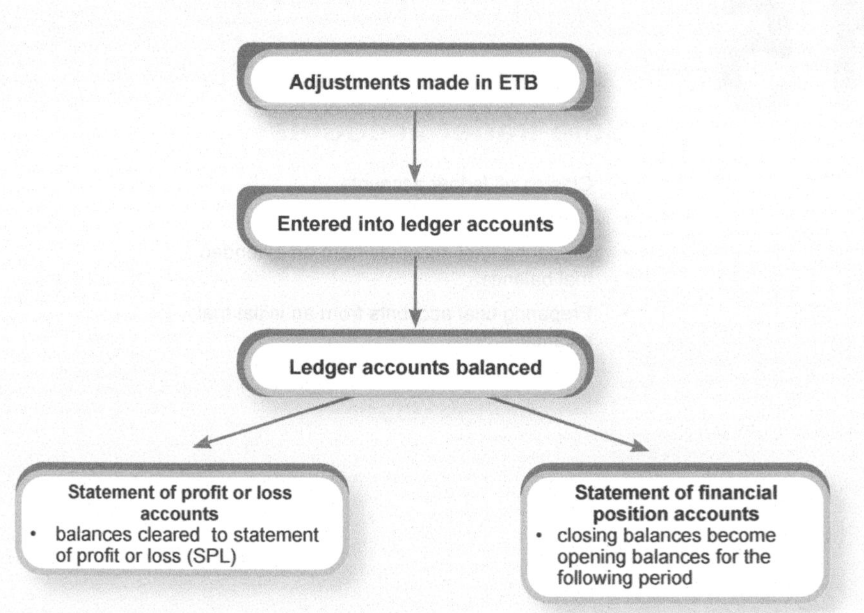

e.g

Example

Year ending 31 December 20X5

Accumulated depreciation account

	£		£
		1 Jan X5 Balance b/d	4,000

The accumulated depreciation account has an opening balance as it is a statement of financial position account.

The depreciation charge account at 1 January 20X5 has no opening balance brought forward.

Depreciation charge for the year ended 31 December 20X5 is £1,000.

Solution

Enter the depreciation charge for the year in the ledger accounts:

Depreciation charge account

	£		£
31 Dec X5 Accum dep'n	1,000	31 Dec X5 SPL	1,000
	1,000		1,000

Accumulated depreciation account

	£		£
31 Dec X5 Balance c/d	5,000	1 Jan X5 Balance b/d	4,000
		31 Dec X5 Depreciation charge	1,000
	5,000		5,000
		1 Jan X6 Balance b/d	5,000

Accumulated account – SFP – balance b/d £5,000

Expense account – SPL – year's expense £1,000

Drawings

Double entry

- sole trader takes money out of his own business for living expenses = drawings.

Double entry:

Debit	Drawings
Credit	Cash

- sole trader take goods out of his own business = drawings.

Double entry:

Debit	Drawings
Credit	Purchases

Accounting treatment

- deduction from capital in the statement of financial position.

Statement of financial position extract

	£
Opening capital	X
Capital introduced in the year	X
Profit/(loss) for the year	X/(X)
Drawings	(X)
Closing capital	X

Preparing final accounts from an extended trial balance

- take final profit or loss column figures and put them into statement of profit or loss account format
- take final statement of financial position column figures and put them in statement of financial position order.

e.g

Example

Extended Trial Balance

Account name	Trial balance		Adjustments		Statement of profit or loss		Statement of financial position	
	DR	CR	DR	CR	DR	CR	DR	CR
	£	£	£	£	£	£	£	£
Sales		40,000				40,000		
Purchases	20,000				20,000			
Inventory at 1 Oct 20X6	2,000				2,000			
Non-current assets at cost	40,000						40,000	
Accumulated depreciation		18,000		6,000				24,000
Receivables ledger control	4,400			400			4,000	
Bank	1,000						1,000	
Payables ledger control		2,500						2,500
Drawings	10,000						10,000	
Capital		28,100						28,100
Rent	2,400			500	1,900			

Example

The ETB from the previous page is continued.

Account name	Trial balance		Adjustments		Statement of profit or loss		Statement of financial position	
	DR	CR	DR	CR	DR	CR	DR	CR
Wages	5,600				5,600			
Heat and light	3,200		300		3,500			
Depreciation charge			6,000		6,000			
Accruals				300				300
Prepayments			500				500	
Irrecoverable debts expense			400		400			
Allowance for doubtful receivables adjustment			200		200			
Allowance for doubtful receivables				200				200
Closing inventory – SFP			2,200				2,200	
Closing inventory – SPL				2,200		2,200		
Net profit					2,600			2,600
	88,600	88,600	9,600	9,600	42,200	42,200	57,700	57,700

Example

Statement of financial position as at 30 September 20X7

	£	£	£
Non-current assets	Cost	Depreciation	Carrying amount
Machinery	40,000	24,000	16,000
	———	———	
Current assets			
Inventory		2,200	
Receivables	4,000		
Less: allowance for doubtful receivables	(200)		
	———		
		3,800	
Prepayments		500	
Bank		1,000	
		———	
		7,500	
Current liabilities			
Payables	2,500		
Accruals	300		
	———	(2,800)	
		———	
Net current assets			4,700
			———
Net assets			20,700
			———
Financed by			
Capital			28,100
Profit for the year			2,600
Less: drawings			(10,000)
			———
			20,700
			———

Alternative presentation format for the statement of financial position:

Example

Statement of financial position as at 30 September 20X7

	£	£	£
Non-current assets	Cost	Depreciation	Carrying amount
Machinery	40,000	24,000	16,000
Current assets			
Inventory		2,200	
Receivables	4,000		
Less: allowance for doubtful receivables	(200)		
		3,800	
Prepayments		500	
Bank		1,000	
			7,500
Total assets			23,500

Capital and liabilities:		£
Capital		28,100
Profit for the year		2,600
Less: drawings		(10,000)
		20,700
Current liabilities:		
Payables	2,500	
Accruals	300	
		2,800
Total capital and liabilities		23,500

Note that the two formats of the statement of financial position show exactly the same information. In the first format, liabilities have been deducted from assets to arrive at net assets which is equal to proprietor's capital.

In the alternative format, non-current and current assets are totalled to show total assets. This is equal to proprietor's capital plus liabilities.

e.g

Example

Statement of profit or loss for the year ended 30 September 20X7

	£	£
Sales		40,000
Cost of goods sold:		
Opening inventory	2,000	
Purchases	20,000	
Closing inventory	(2,200)	
Cost of goods sold		(19,800)
Gross profit		20,200
Add: Sundry income		X
Less:		
Rent	1,900	
Wages	5,600	
Heat and light	3,500	
Depreciation charge	6,000	
Irrecoverable debt expense	400	
Allowance for doubtful receivables adjustment	200	
Total expenses		(17,600)
Profit (loss) for the year		2,600

Preparing final accounts from an initial trial balance

Step 1

Draft journal entries for any adjustments/ errors.

Step 2

Adjust ledger accounts for journal entries.

Step 3

Carry down balances on adjusted ledger accounts.

Step 4

Draw up amended trial balance.

Step 5

Prepare statement of profit or loss and statement of financial position.

Example

The initial trial balance of a sole trader at 30 June 20X6:

	£	£
Sales		40,000
Purchases	20,000	
Inventory at 1 July 20X5	2,000	
Non-current assets at cost	40,000	
Accumulated depreciation at 1 July 20X5		18,000
Receivables ledger control	4,400	
Bank	1,000	
Payables ledger control		2,500
Drawings	10,000	
Capital		28,100
Rent	2,400	
Wages	5,600	
Heat and light	3,200	
	88,600	88,600

The following points are also noted:

(i) Depreciation at 15% straight-line is to be charged for the year

(ii) There is an accrual for electricity of £300

(iii) There is a prepayment for rent of £500

(iv) An irrecoverable debt of £400 is to be written off

(v) An allowance for doubtful receivables of 5% of remaining receivables needs to be set up

(vi) Closing inventory has been valued at £2,200.

Solution

Step 1

Draft journal entries for any adjustments/ errors

(i) Depreciation at 15% straight-line is to be charged for the year

Journal

Debit	Depreciation charge	£6,000
Credit	Accumulated depreciation £40,000 x 15% = £6,000	£6,000

(ii) There is an accrual for electricity of £300

Journal

Debit	Electricity	£300
Credit	Accruals	£300

(iii) There is a prepayment of rent of £500

Journal

Debit	Prepayments	£500
Credit	Rent	£500

(iv) Irrecoverable debt of £400 is to be written off

Journal

Debit	Irrecoverable debts expense	£400
Credit	RLCA	£400

(v) An allowance for doubtful receivables of 5% of remaining receivables needs to be set up

Journal

Debit	Allowance for doubtful receivables adjustment	£200
Credit	Allowance for doubtful receivables	£200

(vi) Closing inventory has been valued at £2,200

Debit Inventory account – SFP	£2,200
Credit Inventory account – SPL	£2,200

Steps 2 and 3

Adjust ledger accounts for journal entries

Carry down balances on adjusted ledger accounts

Accumulated depreciation

	£		£
Balance c/d	24,000	Balance b/d	18,000
		Depreciation charge	6,000
	24,000		24,000
		Balance b/d	24,000

Depreciation charge

	£		£
Accum dep'n	6,000		

Heat and light

	£		£
Balance b/d	3,200	Balance c/d	3,500
Accrual	300		
	3,500		3,500
Balance b/d	3,500		

Accruals

	£		£
		Heat & light	300

Rent

	£		£
Balance b/d	2,400	Prepayment	500
		Balance c/d	1,900
	2,400		2,400
Balance b/d	1,900		

Prepayments

	£		£
Rent	500		

Receivables ledger control

	£		£
Balance b/d	4,400	Irrecoverable debt expense	400
		Balance b/d	4,000
	4,400		4,400
Balance b/d	4,000		

Allowance for doubtul debts

	£		£
Balance c/d	200	Allowance for doubtful receivables adjustment	200
	200		200
		Balance b/d	200

Irrecoverable debts expense

	£		£
RLCA	400		

Allowance for doubtful receivables adjustment

	£		£
Allowance for doubtful receivables	200		

Closing inventory – SPL

	£		£
		Closing inventory SFP	2,200

Closing inventory – SFP

	£		£
Closing inventory SPL	2,200		

Step 4

Draw up amended trial balance

	£	£
Sales		40,000
Purchases	20,000	
Inventory at30 June 20X6	2,000	
Non-current assets at cost	40,000	
Accumulated depreciation at 30 June 20X6		24,000
Receivables ledger control	4,000	
Bank	1,000	
Payables ledger control		2,500
Drawings	10,000	
Capital		28,100
Rent	1,900	
Wages	5,600	
Heat and light	3,500	
Depreciation charge	6,000	

Accruals		300
Prepayments	500	
Irrecoverable debts expense	400	
Allowance for doubtful receivables adjustment	200	
Allowance for doubtful receivables		200
Closing inventory – SFP	2,200	
Closing inventory – SPL		2,200
	97,300	97,300

Step 5

Prepare statement of profit or loss for the year ended 30 June 20X6.

Statement of profit or loss for year ended 30 June 20X6

	£	£
Sales		40,000
Opening inventory	2,000	
Purchases	20,000	
	22,000	
Less: closing inventory	(2,200)	
Cost of goods sold		(19,800)
Gross profit		20,200

Less: expenses		
Rent	1,900	
Wages	5,600	
Heat and light	3,500	
Depreciation charge	6,000	
Irrecoverable debts	400	
Allowance for doubtful debt adjustment	200	
		(17,600)
Profit for year		2,600

Statement of financial position as at 30 June 20X6

	Cost	Dep'n	CA
	£	£	£
Non-current assets	40,000	(24,000)	16,000
Current assets:			
Inventory		2,200	
Receivables	4,000		
Less: allowance for doubtful receivables	(200)		
		3,800	
Prepayments		500	
Bank		1,000	
		7,500	
Current liabilities			
Payables	2,500		
Accruals	300	(2,800)	
Net current assets			4,700
Net assets			20,700
Financed by:			
Capital			28,100
Profit for the year			2,600
Less: drawings			(10,000)
			20,700

CBA focus

In the assessment you will be given an extended trial balance or trial balance and you will be expected to prepare the statement of profit or loss and statement of financial position.

chapter

16

Partnership accounts

- Capital accounts.
- Current accounts.
- Appropriation account.
- Statement of financial position presentation.
- Preparing final accounts for a partnership.

Capital accounts

- one for each partner (generally columnar)
- only generally used when partners pay capital into the business.

Debit Cash/bank

Credit Capital account

Example

A and B have been in partnership for a number of years. A put £30,000 of capital into the business and B put in £20,000.

Capital accounts

	A	B		A	B
	£	£		£	£
			Balance b/d	30,000	20,000

Current accounts

- one for each partner (generally columnar)
- used for transactions between partnership and partners

Current accounts

DEBIT	CREDIT
Drawings	Salaries to partners
Interest on drawings	Sales commission to partners
	Interest on capital
	Profit share

- normally a small credit balance being amount partnership owes to partners.

Example

On 1 January 20X5 A's current account had a balance of £1,000 and B's had a balance of £1,500.

Current accounts

	A	B		A	B
	£	£		£	£
			Balance b/d	1,000	1,500

Appropriation account

- used to share out net profit to partners
- according to profit share agreement.

e.g

Example

During year ended 31 December 20X5 A and B's partnership made a net profit of £48,000.

Partnership agreement

- B to receive salary of £8,000 per annum
- both partners to receive interest on capital balances of 5%
- A and B both receive sales commission of £750
- profit to be split in the ratio of 2:1.

Solution

Appropriation account

	£
Net profit	48,000
Salary – B	(8,000)
Interest on capital	
– A (30,000 x 5%)	(1,500)
– B (20,000 x 5%)	(1,000)
Sales commission	
– A	(750)
– B	(750)
Residual profit	36,000
Share of residual profit	
– A (36,000 x 2/3)	24,000
– B (36,000 x 1/3)	12,000
	36,000

CBA focus

Salaries and sales commission for partners are an appropriation of profit not an expense in the statement of profit or loss.

Calculating interest on capital and interest on drawings will not be required in the assessment, but you will need to understand how to record these items.

- all profit share figures from appropriation account must then be posted to current accounts.

Current accounts

	A	B		A	B
	£	£		£	£
			Balance b/d	1,000	1,500
			Salary		8,000
			Interest on capital	1,500	1,000
			Sales commission	750	750
			Profit share	24,000	12,000

Drawings

- partners take cash out of business

  Debit Current accounts

  Credit Cash/bank

- partners take goods out of the business.

  Debit Current accounts

  Credit Purchases

Example

During the year to 31 December 20X5, A took £25,000 of cash out of the business and B took £20,000 for living expenses.

Current accounts

	A	B		A	B
	£	£		£	£
Drawings	25,000	20,000	Balance b/d	1,000	1,500
			Salary		8,000
			Interest on capital	1,500	1,000
			Sales commission	750	750
			Profit share	24,000	12,000

Statement of financial position presentation

- capital accounts and current accounts balanced
- balances shown in bottom part of statement of financial position.

e.g

Example

Capital accounts

	A	B		A	B
	£	£		£	£
			Balance b/d	30,000	20,000

Current accounts

	A	B		A	B
	£	£		£	£
Drawings	25,000	20,000	Balance b/d	1,000	1,500
			Salary		8,000
			Interest on capital	1,500	1,000
Balance c/d	2,250	3,250	Sales commission	750	750
			Profit share	24,000	12,000
	27,250	23,250		27,250	23,250
			Balance b/d	2,250	3,250

Statement of financial position – extract

	£	£
Total net assets (bal fig)		55,500
Capital		
Capital account – A		30,000
Capital account – B		20,000
		50,000
Current account – A	2,250	
Current account – B	3,250	
		5,500
		55,500

Preparing final accounts for a partnership

Step 1

Prepare the statement of profit or loss – just the same as for a sole trader.

Step 2

Prepare appropriation account and enter profit share in current accounts.

Step 3

Enter drawings in current accounts and balance current accounts.

Step 4

Prepare statement of financial position – just the same as for a sole trader other than the capital section (see on previous page).

Example

C and D have been in partnership for a number of years sharing profits and losses equally and with interest on capital balances at 5% per annum.

Trial balance at 31 December 20X5

	£	£
Sales		75,000
Purchases	32,000	
Inventory at 1 Jan 20X5	3,500	
Non-current assets at cost	60,000	
Accumulated depreciation at 1 Jan 20X5		26,000
Receivables ledger control	7,300	
Allowance for doubtful receivables		300
Bank	2,200	
Payables ledger control		3,800

Drawings – C	12,000	
Drawings – D	11,000	
Capital account – C		20,000
Capital account – D		10,000
Current account – C		2,100
Current account – D		1,700
Rent	3,000	
Advertising	3,800	
Heat and light	4,100	
	138,900	138,900

The following adjustments are to be made:

(i) Depreciation at 10% straight-line is to be charged for the year

(ii) There is an accrual for advertising of £500

(iii) The allowance for doubtful receivables is to be increased to £400

(iv) Closing inventory has been valued at £4,000.

Solution

Step 1

Prepare the statement of profit or loss – just the same as for a sole trader.

C and D Partnership

Statement of profit or loss for the year ended 31 December 20X5

	£	£
Sales		75,000
Opening inventory	3,500	
Purchases	32,000	
	35,500	
Less: closing inventory	(4,000)	
Cost of goods sold		31,500
Gross profit		43,500

Less: expenses		
Rent	3,000	
Advertising (3,800 + 500)	4,300	
Heat and light	4,100	
Depreciation charge (60,000x 10%)	6,000	
Allowance for doubtful debts adjustment (400 – 300)	100	
		(17,500)
Profit		26,000

Step 2

Prepare appropriation account and enter profit share in current accounts.

	£	£
Profit		26,000
Interest on capital –		
C (20,000 x 5%)		(1,000)
D (10,000 x 5%)		(500)
Residual profit		24,500
Profit share –		
C (24,500/2)		12,250
D (24,500/2)		12,250
		24,500

Current accounts

	C	D		C	D
	£	£		£	£
			Balance b/d	2,100	1,700
			Interest	1,000	500
			Profit share	12,250	12,250

Step 3

Enter drawings in current accounts and balance current accounts.

Current accounts

	C	D		C	D
	£	£		£	£
Drawings	12,000	11,000	Balance b/d	2,100	1,700
			Interest	1,000	500
Balance c/d	3,350	3,450	Profit share	12,250	12,250
	15,350	14,450		15,350	14,450
			Balance b/d	3,350	3,450

Step 2

Prepare statement of financial position – just the same as for a sole trader other than the capital section.

Statement of financial position as at 31 December 20X5

	Cost	Dep'n	
	£	£	£
Non-current assets	60,000	32,000	28,000
Current assets:			
Inventory		4,000	
Receivables	7,300		
Less: allowance	(400)		
		6,900	
Bank		2,200	
Total assets		13,100	
Current liabilities			
Payables	3,800		
Accruals	500		
		(4,300)	
Net current assets			8,800
			36,800
Capital account – C		20,000	
Capital account – D		10,000	30,000
Current account – C		3,350	
Current account – D		3,450	6,800
			36,800

chapter

17

Incomplete records

- Introduction.
- Net assets approach.
- Use of control accounts.
- Mark-ups and margins.
- Gross sales margin percentage.
- Assessing the reasonableness of figures.
- Bringing it all together.

Introduction

A business that has incomplete records has failed to keep complete accounting information.

Therefore it is necessary to create a set of key workings as shown in this chapter to prepare the financial statements after establishing the missing figures.

You may need to use these key workings for any task within your assessment.

Net assets approach

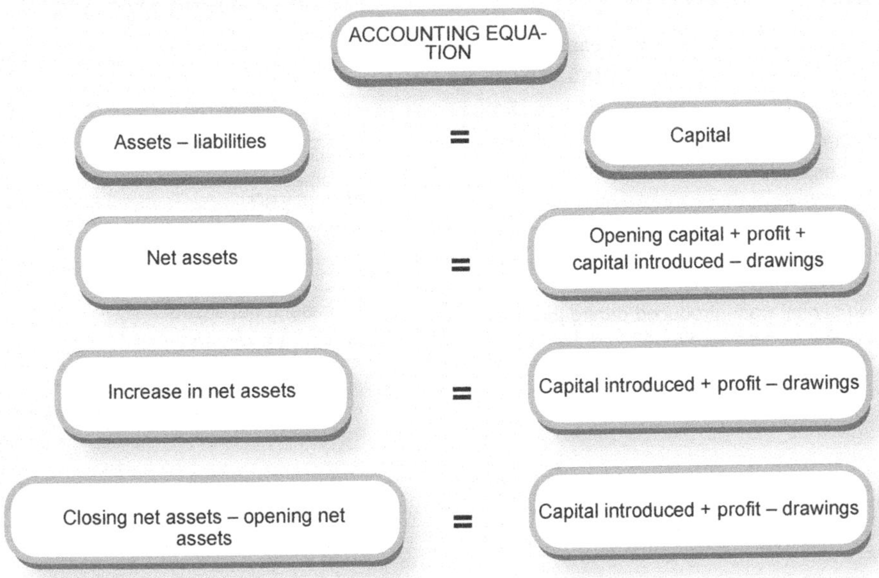

Example

Assets and liabilities of a sole trader:

	1 Jan 20X5 £	31 Dec 20X5 £
Non-current assets (CA)	2,500	3,200
Receivables	1,000	1,600
Payables	(800)	(1,250)
Bank (DEBIT)	600	1,900
Inventory	2,000	2,700

No capital was introduced during the year but the owner took £4,000 in drawings. What was the profit for the year?

Solution

Find value of opening and closing net assets:

	1 Jan 20X5 £	31 Dec 20X5 £
Non-current assets (CA)	2,500	3,200
Receivables	1,000	1,600
Payables	(800)	(1,250)
Bank (DEBIT)	600	1,900
Inventory	2,000	2,700
	5,300	8,150

Increase in net assets =

£8,150 - £5,300 = £2,850

Increase in net assets = Capital introduced + profit − drawings

£2,850 = £0 + profit - drawings

£2,850 + £4,000 = profit

£6,850 = profit

Use of control accounts

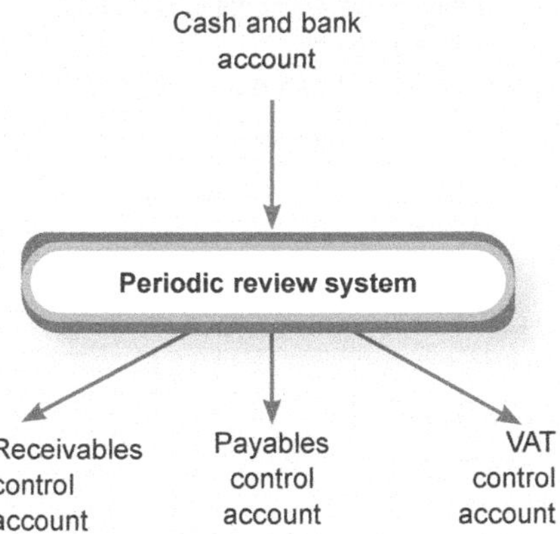

Cash/bank account

- used to find missing figures such as cash takings/cash drawings.

Example

- opening balance on bank account £2,000 positive balance
- opening cash float £200
- banked cash takings of £18,000
- paid expenses out of the bank account of £9,000
- paid cash expenses of £700
- closing bank balance £1,500
- closing cash float £200.

What was the amount of cash takings from customers?

What amount did the owner take out of the bank account as drawings?

Solution

Step 1

Write up both cash and bank accounts from information given.

Step 2

Cash bank account

	Cash	Bank		Cash	Bank
	£	£		£	£
Opening bal	200	2,000	Bankings	18,000	
Bankings		18,000	Expenses	700	9,000
			Closing bal	200	1,500

Look for the missing figures.

In the cash account there is a lot of money going out (bankings/expenses) but nothing coming in. The missing figure here is the amount of cash takings from customers.

In the bank account there is a large amount being banked but less being paid out as expenses. The difference is the amount the owner has taken out as drawings.

Step 3

Balance the accounts to find these missing figures.

Cash bank account

	Cash	Bank		Cash	Bank
	£	£		£	£
Opening bal	200	2,000	Bankings	18,000	
Bankings		18,000	Expenses	700	9,000
Cash takings	**18,700**		Drawings		9,500
			Closing bal	200	1,500
	18,900	20,000		18,900	20,000

Receivables ledger control account

	£		£
Opening balance	X	Bank receipts	X
Sales	X	Discounts allowed	X
		Sales returns	X
		Irrecoverable debts written off	X
		Contra with PLCA	X
		Closing balance	X
	X		X

If three of the four figures are known, the fourth can be found as the balancing figure.

Example

- opening receivables £2,500
- closing receivables £3,400
- cash from sales £30,500

What are the sales for the period?

Solution

Receivables ledger control account

	£		£
Opening balance	2,500	Cash from sales	30,500
Sales (bal fig)	**31,400**	Closing balance	3,400
	33,900		33,900

Example

- opening receivables £12,600
- closing receivables £15,400
- sales £74,000

How much cash was received for sales during the period?

Solution 2

Receivables ledger control account

	£		£
Opening balance	12,600	**Cash from sales**	
Sales	74,000	**(bal fig)**	**71,200**
		Closing balance	15,400
	86,600		86,600

Payables ledger control account

	£		£
Bank payments	X	Opening balance	X
Purchase returns	X	Purchases	X
Discounts received	X		
Contra with RLCA	X		
Closing balance	X		
	X		X

If three of the four figures are known, the fourth can be found as the balancing figure.

Example

- opening payables £1,800
- closing payables £2,200
- cash to suppliers £19,400

What are the purchases for the period?

Solution

Payables ledger control account

	£		£
Cash to suppliers	19,400	Opening balance	1,800
Closing balance	2,200	**Purchases (bal fig)**	**19,800**
	21,600		21,600

Example

- opening payables £18,200
- closing payables £16,100
- purchases £88,200

How much cash was paid to suppliers during the period?

Solution

Payables ledger control account

	£		£
Cash to suppliers (bal fig)	**90,300**	Opening balance	18,200
Closing balance	16,100	Purchases	88,200
	106,400		106,400

VAT

	£		£
		Opening balance	X
Sales returns day book	X	Sales day book	X
Purchase day book	X	Purchase returns day book	X
Cash purchases	X		
		Discounts received daybook	X
Bank - HMRC	X	Cash sales	X
Expenses	X		
Discounts allowed daybook	X		
Irrecoverable debts	X		
Closing balance	X		
	X		X

The opening balance on the VAT account could also be a debit balance at the beginning of the period. This represents a balance owed from HMRC to the business. When balancing the VAT account, either side of the ledger account could be the highest. This is due to the closing balance either being owed to or owed from HMRC at the end of the period.

Example

Given below is the summarised cash book for Joseph, a sole trader, for the year ended 31 March 20X7.

Cash book summary

	£		£
Cash from customers	63,425	Payments to suppliers	28,650
		Payments for expenses	5,800
		HMRC -VAT	3,500
		Drawings	15,450

All sales and purchases made during the year were on credit.

The owner can also provide you with details of the assets and liabilities at the start and at the end of the year as follows:

	1 April 20X6	31 March 20X7
	£	£
RLCA	10,500	11,200
PLCA	6,200	7,500
Sales tax	4,200 CR	?

(i) What is the sales revenue figure for the year?

(ii) What is the purchases figure for the year?

(iii) What is the closing balance on the VAT account? Round your VAT figures down to the nearest whole £.

Solution

(i) Complete the receivables ledger control account to show the amount of sales revenue for the year.

Step 1
Write up the receivables ledger control account from the information given.

Step 2
Balance the receivables ledger control account by totalling the credit side of the account.

RLCA

Detail	£	Detail	£
Balance b/d	10,500	Cash received	63,425
Sales revenue (bal fig)	64,125	Balance c/d	11,200
	74,625		74,625

Step 3
The sales revenue for the year is the balancing figure on the debit side.

(ii) Complete the payables ledger control account to show the amount of purchases made during the year.

Step 1
Write up the payables ledger control account from the information given.

Step 2
Balance the payables ledger control account by totalling the debit side of the account.

PLCA

Detail	£	Detail	£
Cash payments	28,650	Balance b/d	6,200
Balance c/d	7,500	Purchases (bal fig)	29,950
	36,150		36,150

Step 3
The purchases for the year is the balancing figure on the credit side.

(iii) Complete the VAT account to show the balance carried down at 31 March 20X7.

Step 1
Write up the VAT account from the information given. Note: VAT on both sales and purchases will need to be calculated using the answers to parts (i) and (ii) of the example.

Step 2
Balance the VAT account by totalling the credit side of the account.

VAT

Detail	£	Detail	£
VAT on purchases (£29,950 / 6)	4,991	Balance b/d	4,200
Bank – HMRC	3,500	VAT on sales (£64,125 / 6)	10,687
Balance c/d	6,396		
	14,887		14,887

Step 3
The closing balance on the VAT account is the balancing figure on the debit side.

Mark-ups and margins

- cost structures provide a link between selling price and cost.

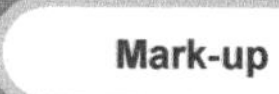

Mark-up	Margins
% added to cost to find selling price	gross profit as a % of selling price

Example

Find the cost structure for:

- mark-up of 20%
- margin of 20%

	Mark-up		Margin
	%		%
Sales	120	Sales	100
Cost of goods sold	(100)	Cost of goods sold	(80)
Gross profit	20	Gross profit	20

Using cost structures

- if the cost structure is known together with either selling price or cost of goods sold, the other figure can be found.

Example

Mark-up

Goods with a selling price of £30,000 are sold at a mark-up of 25%.What was their cost?

Solution

Cost structure:

	%	£	Working
Sales	125	30,000	
Cost of goods sold	(100)	24,000	(30,000 x 100/125)
Gross profit	25		

Gross sales margin percentage

The gross sales profit margin percentage shows the percentage of profit retained from the selling price after deducting the cost of producing that good or service. This can be calculated as:

$$\frac{\text{Gross Profit}}{\text{Sales}} \times 100$$

In the examination, after calculating the cost of goods sold using either mark-up or margin, you may then be asked to calculate a component of cost of goods sold, for example, opening or closing inventory.

Example

Margin

A business sells goods at a margin of 25%. During the period sales were £50,000. What is the figure for cost of goods sold?

Solution

Cost structure:

	%	£	Working
Sales	100	50,000	
Cost of goods sold	(75)	37,500	50,000 x 75/100
Gross profit	25		

Assessing the reasonableness of figures

Accountants should ensure that they are applying professional scepticism when assessing the reasonableness of figures provided in a given context.

Professional scepticism is an attitude that includes a questioning mind, being alert to conditions which may indicate possible misstatement due to error.

This should be taken into account when using the approaches to incomplete records, outlined in this chapter.

Bringing it all together

CBA focus

In the examination a typical incomplete records scenario is where you are given some asset/liability details together with a summarised bank account.

You are then asked to find sales, purchases and other expenses.

Example

John is a sole trader and prepares his accounts to 30 September 20X8.The summary of his bank account is as follows.

	£		£
Balance b/d 1 Oct 20X7	40,000	Postage	3,000
Receipts from receivables	80,000	General expenses	10,000
		Rent	10,000
		Payments to payables	30,000
		Drawings	12,000
		Balance at 30 Sept 20X8	55,000
	120,000		120,000

Receivables at 1 October 20X7 were £30,000 and at 30 September 20X8 were £40,000.

Payables at 1 October 20X7 were £20,000 and at 30 September 20X8 were £25,000.

Rent was paid at £2,000 per quarter. Rent had not been paid for the final quarter to 30 September 20X7 of the previous period.

During the year to 30 September 20X8 total payments of £3,000 for electricity were made which covered the period 1 September 20X7 to 30 November 20X8. You may assume that this cost was incurred evenly each month. Electricity is included in general expenses.

Example

Task 1

Calculate the capital at 1 October 20X7.

Task 2

Prepare the receivables ledger control account for the year ended 30 September 20X8, showing credit sales as the balancing figure.

Task 3

Prepare the payables ledger control account for the year ended 30 September 20X8, showing credit purchases as the balancing figure.

Task 4

Prepare the rent account for the year ended 30 September 20X8.

Task 5

Prepare the general expenses account for the year ended 30 September 20X8.

Task 6

Prepare a trial balance at 30 September 20X8.

Solution

Task 1

Capital at 1 October 20X7

	£
Bank	40,000
Receivables	30,000
Payables	(20,000)
Rent accrued	(2,000)
Electricity accrued	(200)
Capital	47, 800

Tutorial note. Remember that capital equals net assets. You therefore have to list all the assets and liabilities at the start of the year to find the net assets and therefore the capital.

Example

Task 2

Receivables ledger control account

	£		£
Balance b/d 1 Oct 20X7	30,000	Cash from receivables	80,000
Credit sales (bal fig)	90,000	Bal c/d 30 Sept X8	40,000
	120,000		120,000

Task 3

Payables ledger control account

	£		£
Payments to payables	30,000	Balance b/d 1 Oct 20X7	20,000
Balance c/d 30 Sept 20X8	25,000	Purchases (bal fig)	35,000
	55,000		55,000

Task 4

Rent account

	£		£
Bank	10,000	Balance b/d 1 Oct 20X7	2,000
		Expense for the year - SPL	8,000
	10,000		10,000

Example

Task 5

General expenses account

	£		£
Bank	10,000	Balance b/d 1 Oct 20X7	200
		Expense for the year - SPL	9,400
		Prepayment c/d (2/15 x £3,000)	400
	10,000		10,000

Tutorial note. The £3,000 paid in the year for electricity to 30 September 20X8 covers 15 months. £200 is for the month of September 20X7 (an accrual) and £400 is for the two months October and November 20X8 (a prepayment).

Example

Task 6

Trial balance as at 30 September 20X8

	£	£
Capital at 1 October 20X7		47,800
Bank	55,000	
Sales		90,000
Receivables ledger control a/c	40,000	
Purchases	35,000	
Payables ledger control a/c		25,000
Prepayment – general expenses	400	
Rent	8,000	
General expenses	9,400	
Postage	3,000	
Drawings	12,000	
	162,800	162,800

e.g

Example

Given below is the summarised bank account of a sole trader for the year ended 31 December 20X5.

Bank account

	£		£
Opening balance	1,300	Payables	25,400
Receivables	41,500	Expenses	4,700
		Drawings	10,000
		Closing balance	2,700
	42,800		42,800

Other assets and liabilities were as follows:

	1 Jan 20X5 £	31 Dec 20X5 £
Non-current assets at cost	10,000	10,000
Accumulated depreciation	4,000	not yet available
Receivables	2,000	3,800
Payables	1,600	2,200
Inventory	1,000	1,500
Accruals for expenses	500	600
Capital	8,200	not yet available

Depreciation is charged at 10% on the straight-line basis.

Task

Produce the trial balance at 31 December 20X5.

Solution

Find sales for the year.

Receivables ledger control account

	£		£
Opening balance	2,000	Cash from	
Sales (bal fig)	43,300	customers (Bank)	41,500
		Closing balance	3,800
	45,300		45,300

Find purchases for the year.

Payables ledger control account

	£		£
Cash to		Opening balance	1,600
suppliers (Bank)	25,400	Purchases	26,000
Closing balance	2,200	(bal fig)	
	27,600		27,600

Calculate the expenses for the year.

Expenses

	£		£
Cash paid (Bank)	4,700	Opening accrual	500
Closing accrual	600	Expenses	
		(bal fig)	4,800
	5,300		5,300

Calculate the depreciation charge for the year.

Depreciation = £10,000 x 10%
= £1,000

Calculate the updated accumulated depreciation at the year-end.

Accumulated depreciation = £4,000
+ £1,000
= £5,000

Prepare the sole trader's trial balance at 31 December 20X5.

	DR	CR
	£	£
Non-current assets (from assets/liabilities list)	10,000	
Accumulated depreciation (calculation)		5,000
Depreciation charge (calculation)	1,000	
Sales (calculation)		43,300
Purchases (calculation)	26,000	
Bank (from bank account)	2,700	
Drawings (from bank account)	10,000	
Receivables (from RLCA)	3,800	
Payables (from total PLCA)		2,200
Accruals (from assets/liabilities list)		600
Expenses (calculation)	4,800	
Inventory (opening inventory)	1,000	
Closing inventory – SFP	1,500	
Closing inventory – SPL		1,500
Capital (opening capital)		8,200
	60,800	60,800

chapter

18

Interpretation of profitability ratios

- Overview.
- Uses of ratios.
- Profitability ratios.
- Limitations of ratio analysis.

Overview

This chapter deals with the topics involved in 'interpretation of accounts'. This includes:

- the uses of profitability ratios.
- the calculation and meaning of profitability ratios.
- the limitations of ratio analysis.

Uses of ratios

Key Point

- Ratio analysis is a means of interpreting financial statements.
- Users will review the financial statements and make decisions based on the information given. Ratios are calculated and compared with:
  - the performance of the business in previous years
  - the budgeted or planned performance in the current year
  - the performance of similar businesses.
- Ratios can assist in pointing the user of the financial statements to areas where the company may be performing particularly well or badly. They do not in themselves provide an answer but they can help in indicating the right direction for further investigation.

Profitability ratios

CBA focus

Ratios are important tools to assist in the interpretation of financial statements. You must learn these ratios and be able to calculate and interpret them as an exam task may require you to do both.

Gross profit margin

The gross profit margin is calculated as:

$$\frac{\text{Gross profit}}{\text{Sales revenue}} \times 100$$

Gross profit represents the difference between sales revenue and cost of sales. The gross profit margin works out the proportion of sales revenue that becomes gross profit. The margin works this out in percentage terms on an average basis across all sales for the year.

Net profit margin

The net profit margin is calculated as:

$$\frac{\text{Profit for the year}}{\text{Sales revenue}} \times 100$$

Net profit represents the difference between sales revenue and all costs i.e. the overall profit made for the year. The net profit margin is an expansion of the gross profit margin and includes all of the expenses and other items that come after gross profit.

Return on capital employed (ROCE)

ROCE measures how much net profit is generated for every £1 capital invested in the business.

$$\text{ROCE} = \frac{\text{Profit for the year}}{\text{Capital employed}} \times 100$$

Where capital employed = capital + non-current liabilities.

Expense over revenue percentage

The expense over revenue percentage is calculated to show the relationship between an individual expense or a group of expenses and sales revenue.

It is calculated as:

$$\frac{\text{Expense}}{\text{Sales revenue}} \times 100$$

Limitations of ratio analysis

- Ratios do not provide answers; they merely highlight significant features or trends in the financial statements. They usually highlight areas that need further investigation.
- Be mindful of seasonal trade as accounting year-ends are often just after the seasonal trend is over when the business is at its best.
- Watch out for window dressing in the financial statements such as collecting receivables just before the year-end in order to show a larger cash balance and lower receivables than is normal.
- Accounting ratios are based on accounting information and are only as accurate as that underlying accounting information.
- If comparisons are to be made they must be with companies with a similar trade, otherwise the pattern of ratios will be different and the comparisons meaningless.

Index

A

Accounting equation 7
Accruals 97, 98
Accruals concept 32, 98
Appropriation account 151
Asset 7

B

Balancing ledger accounts 12
Bank reconciliation 95, 96

C

Capital 7
Capital accounts 150
Capital expenditure 26
Cash 9, 27
Casting error 108
Compensating errors 109
Contra entry 83
Control accounts 163
Correcting errors 112
Credit 8, 10, 14
Current accounts 150

D

Debit 8, 14
Depreciation 31, 32, 33, 35
Diminishing-balance method 34
Disposals 42
Double-entry bookkeeping 6
Doubtful receivables 69, 70, 72, 77
Drawings 134, 150, 152
Dual effect 6

E

Errors 107, 108, 109
Errors of commission 109
Errors of omission 109
Errors of original entry 109
Errors of principle 109
Expense over revenue 186
Extended trial balance 51, 52, 53, 117, 118, 135
Extraction error 108

G

General allowance 77
Gross profit margin 185

I

IAS 2 Inventory 66
IAS 16 Property, plant and equipment 26
Income accrued 104
Income prepaid 104
Incomplete records 159
Intangible 30
Inventory 62
Irrecoverable debts 69, 70, 71

J

Journal entries 107

L

Ledger accounts 8, 132
Liability 7
Limitations of ratio analysis 186
Loan 27

M

Margins 172
Mark-ups 172

N

Net assets approach 161
Net profit margin 185
Net realisable value 67
Non-current asset register 28, 29, 49
Non-current assets 25, 26, 30

P

Part-exchange 27, 44
Partnership accounts 149
Payable 7
Payables ledger control account 83
Payroll 23
Prepayments 101
Profitability ratios 185
Property, plant and equipment 26, 27

R

Ratios 184
Receivable 7
Receivables ledger control account 82
Reconciliations 84, 89
Residual value 33
Return on capital employed 185
Revenue expenditure 26

S

Separate entity 6
Single entry 108
Sole trader accounts 131
Specific allowance 77
Statement of financial position 52, 59, 132, 153
Statement of profit or loss 52, 132
Straight-line method 33
Suspense 111, 114
Suspense account 107

T

Tangible 30
Transposition error 108
Trial balance 14, 52, 109, 140

U

Uncleared lodgements 96
Unpresented cheques 96
Useful life 33
Users of final accounts 56

V

VAT 17, 18, 19, 20